The Jackie Robinson Story

(1917-1972)

Written in Two Parts by

Alan Troilett & Eric Brodie

The Jackie Robinson Story

ISBN 0 9547264 2 1

Printed in 2004 by Pickard Communication

Published & Printed by Pickard Communication
10-11 Riverside Park
Sheaf Gardens
Sheffield S2 4BB
Telephone 0114 275 7222 or 275 7444
email info@picomm.co.uk
www picomm.co.uk

This work is dedicated to the kindest, sincere
and most beautiful woman in the world,
my mother-in-law,
Lillian Robinson

Alan Troilett

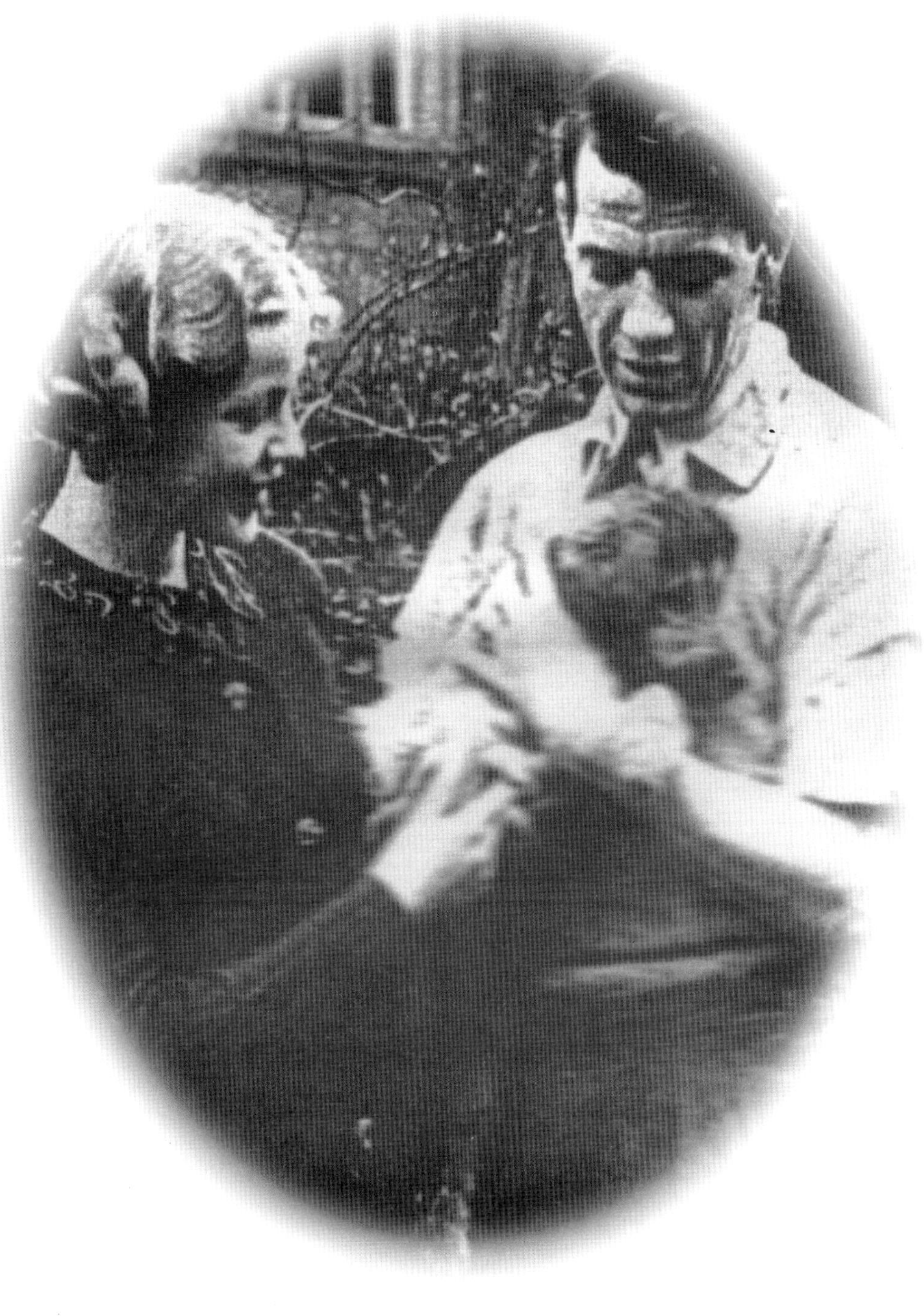

Preface.

This book has been written in two parts.

PART ONE tells you all about the personal life of Jackie Robinson, the football mad youngster from Shiremore, the love for his wife Lillian, his family and friends, all his heartaches, his triumphs, and the ups and downs on and off the football field. All these chapters of this great Sheffield Wednesday and England International inside right and great Hillsborough legend, could only have been written by someone very close to Jackie, his son in law ***Alan Troilett.***

Alan is 68 years old and a retired senior estimator on Trident submarines. He participated in Rugby Union, playing for Liverpool Sefton, until he was 39. He met his wife, Yvonne, Jackie Robinson's daughter, while singing country and western, which he did on a semi-professional basis. It was only after they married that Alan found Yvonne had a famous father. He then visited Hillsborough and met many of Jackie's old fans. One of these fans was Eric Brodie who had long been an admirer of Jackie Robinson, and who expressed a desire to be involved in this book.

PART TWO of this book has been written and compiled by a lifelong fan of Jackie Robinson.

Although born in Shoreham Street, two minutes walk from Bramall Lane, the home of Sheffield United Football club, this eight year old lad heard the magic name "Jackie Robinson" and never stopped thinking or talking about him for almost the next sixty-two years. My name is Eric Brodie and I am very proud to say, I was that lad.

I had wanted to try and put a book together about Sheffield Wednesday, but I thought at that time that I might have been stretching my capabilities. A few years later a Wednesday book came out and I was devastated for not having a go. In 1990 I started to write my life story, which was going to include lots of football, having been going to watch Sheffield United from just before the war and Wednesday from around 1943. I saw lots of great players from both Sheffield and visiting teams, players I will never forget. I wanted to write about them all because in those years up to 1960 football was a big part in my life. In 1993 my lovely wife Barbara passed away so the book I was hoping to write got pushed to one side.

I have not yet met Alan Troilett. but having the chance to communicate with him and Jackie's wife Lillian we were able to enjoy many phone conversations speaking of our respect and adoration of this lovely man. We talked about the great footballer he was and the hero worship he so richly deserved.

It was then that Alan told me that he was hoping to write a book about Jackie's life so I asked him to order three copies for me. I was really thrilled at the idea of a book about my lifelong hero being wrote. I told Allen I was going to write quite a lot about Jackie in the book I had started but had sadly shelved To my complete joy and surprise Alan said "let's put our material together and do a book". I could not believe it Alan sent me his contribution, which is part one of this book. Jackie's wife Lillian passed away before this book was published. This saddened me very much as I had also missed the invitation I had been kindly offered to spend time at her home in Whitley Bay.

Alan is dedicating this book to Lillian Robinson, Jackie's wife, his love, and truly his greatest admirer.

Eric Brodie

CONTENTS

PART ONE

by Alan Troilett

The Jackie Robinson Story

(1917-1972)

Once upon a time in the village of Shiremoor

there was born a boy named

Jackie Robinson.

If this sounds like the start of a fairy tale

it is meant to be.

As in all fairy tales, there has to be a hero,

to many people Jackie was that hero.

Chapter One
Roar of the Crowd

There are many forms of entertainments: - cinema, theatre, pop concerts, indoor sports, and outdoor sports. Of all the outdoor sports: - cricket, tennis, baseball, rugby league, and football, the last is surely the most popular around the world.

From the cobbled streets of Northern England, through the hard dirt, dusty plains of Africa, South America and Australia to the lush playing fields of some of the world's richest countries, children have been brought up to appreciate football. Village plays village, town plays town; there are football leagues all over the world, and country plays country.

Only the very talented get chosen to play for their country, other mere mortals become one of the crowd. Football crowds are usually in two sections: the home crowd supports the home team and usually has the same spot in the ground, match after match, year after year. The away crowd travels the country and even the world to support its team, and its own particular heroes. Some use clapperboards, some use drums, but most of all they use their voices. When the game is at its most exciting this noise becomes almost deafening - roar of the crowd.

When the players are in the dressing room they can hear a dull buzzing noise, the spectators are preparing for the event, as kick off time comes near, the players line up outside the dressing room and approach the tunnel. It is a frightening experience entering that tunnel knowing that even though it is a team game, everyone in the crowd can see if you are playing well or not.

Jackie had his first experience of such a roar coming out of the tunnel at West Bromwich Albion and he was 17 years old.

Chapter Two
Jackie The Youngster

Clip, clop, clip, clop was the sound that young Jackie woke up to each morning. The miners in the village community of Shiremoor were going to work; Shiremoor was a village to the northeast of Newcastle upon Tyne, a famous footballing city.

He was a shy lad, his mother and father had another son and two daughters, and they were a hard working, church going family. He was born on August 10th 1917.

School was easy for him because he excelled at sport. He was a champion athlete, and played both rugby and football for his school team. He got a county schoolboy cap in 1930 at the age of 13.

Jackie Robinson wearing his county cap

He loved football and joined West Wylam F.C. which was a junior pit team in the Newcastle area. Although he was one of the youngest members of the team, he was soon making a name for himself as a fast, tricky inside forward.

Jackie had many good friends, being good at sport made him a target for hangers on. Yes, even at that young age children feel important being around a celebrity, for that was what young Jackie was becoming.

Being a good-looking lad he was not without female admirers. Two school classes below was a beautiful young girl, Lillian Casson. Note that name for in later years Jackie and Lillian were to become one of the romances of the century.

One day in 1934, Bill Walker the former Aston Villa and English international who was now manager of Sheffield Wednesday, came to watch a wing half that was marking Jackie. The wing half was made to look very ordinary, Jackie played brilliant.

Mr Walker was so impressed that he obtained Jackie's' parents consent, because he was under 16, for the lad to join the ground staff at Sheffield Wednesday.

Looking back I don't know who would have been the most excited, Jackie for joining a first division team; or Billy for taking to Hillsborough a young talent that was a natural skilled footballer, who might one day play for England as he himself had done. Yes, Bill Walker was very proud of that day's work.

Chapter Three

Sheffield Wednesday's days (pre-war)

The 1934-1935 season treated Sheffield Wednesday well, they finished 3rd in the league and were in the final of the F.A. cup at Wembley to play West Bromwich Albion. Wednesday had two English internationals in their line-up, Ted Catlin and Ronnie Starling.

Jackie enjoyed training and certainly impressed the manager, for he hadn't even played for the 2nd team when he was told he was travelling to West Bromwich to watch. This was on April 22nd 1935, five days later the two teams were to meet again in the cup final.

'Get your clothes off lad, you're playing', the manager said, just 30 minutes before kick off. Billy Walker was resting Ronnie Starling, the international; there was no time for nerves. Because of the secrecy, no boots had been taken for Jackie. 'As I am taking Ronnie Starling's place, I'll play in his boots.' That was a daring thing to say, he played inside left and scored a goal on his debut. They drew 1-1. The boots pinched a bit, but scoring a goal in your first game in the English first division eases any discomfort that may otherwise have been felt. As they say, you can't keep a good man down. Five days later, Jackie was on the hallowed turf at Wembley, granted this time he was smartly dressed in blazer and slacks, but he was part of the squad. What an honour for a 17 year old. Sheffield Wednesday won 4-2. Jackie's' photo is in the lounge at Hillsborough with that squad of 1934-35.

Sheffield Wednesday players strolling around Wembley before the 1935 FA Cup Final. Left to right: Burrows, Surtees, Brown, Palethorpe, Sharp, Irwin (trainer), Billy Walker and 17 year old Jackie Robinson far right

Jackie was used sparingly throughout the 1935-36 season he played in only five games. Because of his age, the manager Billy Walker did not want him to play too often against seasoned veterans. His first home game for Sheffield Wednesday was Chelsea and his team won 4-1, not bad for young Jackie.

The 1936-37 season was remarkable, after just 19 games the English international trial presented itself to him. He was taking the first division by storm and had already scored 6 goals.

On March 17th 1937 St Patrick's day at Burnley, Jackie played for the possibles against the probables. Ted Catlin one of his Sheffield Wednesday team mates, a senior, player at Sheffield and an established international, was defending against him. This did not deter young Jackie, still only just turned 19. He rose to the occasion and indeed must have impressed the selectors because just two months later he was selected to play against Finland on May 20th 1937 at Helsinki. He was 19 years, 9 months old.

Ted Catlin, a Sheffield Wednesday team mate who was already an England international

Whenever the name of Jackie Robinson comes up, for some annoying reason comes the question of Jackie's age. To me it is a sin that nearly all the sports reporters of the day got it wrong. Several claim that Jackie was 17 years 3 months old when he won his cap. Why didn't they check up on the age factor? Later on when Duncan Edwards of Manchester United got his first cap at the age of 18 years 6 months I am sure a proper check was carried out on his age. Even so, what does it matter? Jackie was still a young lad of 19 years 9 months. Apparently his mother had mistakenly got his age mixed up with his brother Frankie. However, I am sure that politics came into this in later years, by giving his age as two years younger Sheffield Wednesday stood to make more money. After all Jackie would have two extra seasons to play for whoever he was being transferred to. Jackie certainly knew his age; it was on his marriage certificate in 1938.

John Robinson, Sheffield Wednesday regular and England international - all achieved before his 20th birthday

Even with all the brilliance of their young inside right, Sheffield Wednesday were relegated and started the 1937-38 season in division 2.

This league was no mug league, teams such as West Ham United, Sheffield United, Newcastle United, Tottenham Hotspurs and Manchester United were all playing in it. With a phenomenal body swerve and an ability to score goals, Jackie was the type of player much sought after. Several clubs were after Jackie to sign for them, including Arsenal, West Bromwich Albion and Preston North End. Ted Caltin's name was also being mentioned in transfer talks. Luckily however the financial side was not so much in the club's mind as an all-round strengthening of the team.

In 29 games, 7 goals assured Jackie of going on the England team's continental tour to Germany, Switzerland and France. In a later chapter I will deal with his tour.

INTERNATIONAL FOOTBALLER WEDS

ISS LILIAN CASSON, of Shiremoor, signing the register after er marriage to Mr. John Robinson, Sheffield Wednesday iternational forward, at Killingworth Parish Church, to-day.

Miss Lillian Casson of Shiremoor, signing the register after her marriage to John (Jackie) Robinson the Sheffield Wednesday and England International at Killingworth Parish Church

During the season, Jackie had been travelling from his digs in Sheffield up to his beloved Tyneside whenever he got the opportunity to see Lily, his school-day girl friend. At the beginning of the 1938-39 season they married on a Wednesday, very appropriate for a Wednesday player.

Ten days later Jackie was to play for England against Wales at Cardiff. He and Lillian settled down in a lovely house near to the ground in Sheffield. Jackie used to go off training and Lillian soon became domesticated, cooking for her young international footballer.

Jackie was enjoying all this sudden fame even though he was basically shy. He got on very well with all his teammates. They all played golf together and he used to play table soccer with Ronnie Starling and darts with Charlie Napier.

They finished 3rd in division 2. Jackie scored 15 goals in 37 league matches and 4 goals out of 8 F.A. cup games.

In September 1938, he was called to represent the English football league against Ireland at Belfast. Sadly the World War II was to bring an end to his international career.

Chapter Four

Sheffield Wednesday – The war years and later

Up until now Jackie had scored 33 goals in 110 games. The war years saw him score 91 in 109 games. With a further 6 from 9 games after the war. A total of 130 goals for Sheffield Wednesday out of 228 games. He was a lethal goal machine; his rate of 1 goal every 1.75 games or 4 goals every 7 games wants some beating.

Robinson. J was stationed at Middlesbrough for most of his war service. Whenever he got permission to leave his unit he would be playing for Sheffield Wednesday.

Because of the war and for ease of travelling the F.A. brought in regional leagues instead of the division 1, 2 etc.

For just one season, 1939-40, Sheffield Wednesday played in the East Midlands region division. They only played three games in division 2 before war broke out. I must say I am quite impressed with the efficient way the change over was done. September 2nd 1939 - division 2; October 21st 1939 - East Midlands region division.

His army duties only enabled Jackie to play 2 games in this East Midlands region division.

In 1940-41 Sheffield Wednesday played in the North Regional league. Jackie was only able to play on 9 occasions, scoring 7 times.

The 1941-42 season saw him score 7 goals in 8 games. He had been working hard in the army and was promoted to the rank of corporal.

SNAPSHOTS OF THE PLAYERS *continued.*

DODDS. Centre-forward. The one-time Sheffield United favourite. Joined Blackpool in 1939 and is cracking goals for them in wartime football, just as he did for United, who got him for a song from Huddersfield Town. One of football's £10,000 stars: a Scottish International. Has scored 44 goals for Blackpool this season. Like several other members of the team, is in the R.A.F.

FINAN. Inside right. A brilliant player, who has rendered the club yeoman service for several seasons. Dangerous anywhere near goal with both head and foot. Born at Old Kilpatrick.

BURBANKS. Outside left. Brilliant winger of Sunderland, whom he helped to win the F.A. Cup in 1937. Played for Doncaster in wartime football for a spell before being moved to the seaside. A native of Bentley, he played for Thorne Town and Denaby, who transferred him to Sunderland.

TEAMS FOR TO-DAY

SHEFFIELD WEDNESDAY

Colours: BLUE & WHITE VERTICAL STRIPES; BLACK KNICKERS.

Right Wing — Left Wing

MORTON

2 ASHLEY 3 GADSBY

4 RUSSELL 5 MILLERSHIP 6 COCKROFT

7 REYNOLDS 8 ROBINSON 9 F. MELLING 10 THOMPSON 11 SWIFT

Referee: Mr. F. W. WORT (Liverpool).

Linesmen: Mr. H. BERRY (Huddersfield). (Blue & White Flag) Mr. W. MARTIN (Leeds). (Red & White Flag)

11 BURBANKS 10 FINAN 9 DODDS 8 DIX 7 GARDNER

6 JOHNSTON 5 HAYWARD 4 FARROW

3 HUBBICK 2 POPE

SAVAGE

Left Wing — Right Wing

BLACKPOOL

Colours: TANGERINE JERSEYS, WHITE KNICKERS.

"Story of the Football League"

Is still available at Pre-War Price of

10s. 6d. (plus Postage 9d.)

From

THE FOOTBALL LEAGUE OFFICES.

102, FISHERGATE,

PRESTON.

8th MAY, 1943. PRICE TWOPENCE.

Football League (War) Cup

FINAL.

SHEFFIELD WEDNESDAY GROUND,

SATURDAY, 8th MAY, 1943.

KICK-OFF 3.15 p.m.

SHEFFIELD WEDNESDAY

VERSUS

BLACKPOOL

Official Programme.

The War time Cup Final 1943 programme for the Home game against Blackpool FC. Jackie notched the only Wednesday goal

The War time Cup Final 1943. Jackie meeting the Lord of the Admiralty.

By the 1942-43 season Jackie was at his peak and scored 35 goals in 32 games, 16 were in 14 games in the football league (North), 19 were in 8 games in the league North (cup).

Sheffield Wednesday finished 3rd out of 48 clubs in the league; and 5th out of 54 clubs in the North cup qualifying competition. They played Blackpool in the final. This was a two legged home and away final. They drew 2-2 at Blackpool, Robinson scoring one of the goals. They lost 1-2 at Sheffield, again Robinson scored.

The Army Cup Final winners with Jackie Robinson 2nd player from left on front row.

February 20th 1943 Jackie Robinson was chosen to play for the England army against the Scotland army at Glasgow.

Of course after getting 6 hat tricks that season, how could the selectors leave him out.

1943-44 season saw Jackie score 12 goals in 8 games – again in the football league (North)

1944-45 season he scored 12 goals in 16 games – football league north.

1945-46 season he scored 17 goals in 21 games – football league north.

He must surely have been the highest scorer in the football league north, having scored 71 goals in 86 games. This should be one for the Guinness book of records.

Sheffield derbies were always well attended and Jackie was a thorn in the side for United. In 21 derby games he scored 17 goals, again I think this is worthy of a mention in the record book.

The local newspaper 'The Star' used to give a dinner to honour its two football teams, at the Grand Hotel in Sheffield in May. Wednesday are the blue and whites and United the red and whites. At one of the dinners Jackie very undiplomatically wore a red and white striped tie that he owned; it caused quite a stir.

He played in lots of army representative games to aid the war effort. He was featured in a coaching book published by the Football Association, showing how to pass a man and he could certainly do that.

Alex James, the great Arsenal international when writing about Jackie, linked Robinson to David Jack with his quick burst through the opposition's defence.

Other reporters said he was the fastest inside forward ever seen. One of England's finest ever inside forwards.

To me his record speaks for itself.

Chapter Five
The International Player

For the boy from Shiremoor travelling by steam train to Sheffield was an adventure. It was very exciting being chosen to play for the possibles against the probables. He would be playing among legends and famous names he had only read about. Granted he was gradually meeting a few of these great footballers in his games for Sheffield, but the thoughts of being at Burnley among these stars made him nervous. Ted Catlin his teammate would be with him, but Ted had told him to expect no mercy. He was an established international of the last three England games. He would be playing against Jackie. Just play your normal game Jackie, forget names, they mean nothing when you have the ball at your feet.

The possibles team consisted of; - Tweedy (Grimsby Town); Sproston (Leeds United); Barkas (Manchester City) (Capt); Jobling (Charlton Athletic); Cullis (Wolverhampton Wanderers); Welsh (Charlton Athletic); Mathews (Stoke City); Robinson (Sheffield Wednesday); Payne (Luton Town); Goulden (West Ham United); Johnson (Stoke City).

The probables team consisted of; - Woodley (Chelsea); Male (Arsenal) (Capt); Catlin (Sheffield Wednesday); Britton (Everton); Young (Huddersfield Town); Bray (Manchester City); Kirchen (Arsenal); Bowden (Arsenal); Steele (Stoke City); Westwood (Bolton Wanderers); Brook (Manchester City).

As you will see fourteen out of the twenty-two players were from the North or Midlands, hence the selection of Burnley as the venue. The referee and linesmen were all from Lancashire.

The footballers in those days did not get the astronomical sums that they get in modern game.

I think today's footballers are grossly overpaid, and the size of transfer fees ridiculous.

Jackie Robinson would have been a very wealthy man in these days,. As it was, he got 10 shillings a week for playing, 50p in new coinage. Much depended on the policy of the selectors, who were to meet on April 12th. The previous year they did not select one player who had taken part in the trial match.

Ted Catlin in direct opposition to Jackie, in the probables versus the possibles

Jackie did not get selected for the game against Scotland on April 17th. However he did get his first cap against Finland on May 20th 1937 in Helsinki. England won 8-0 and he scored a goal. Playing well and scoring made it a dream debut.

The England team that day consisted of; - Woodley; Male; Hapgood; Willingham; Betmead; Copping; Kirchen; Robinson; Paine; Steele and Johnson.

At the end of the 1937-1938 season, Jackie was selected to tour the continent with the England team.

The first game was on May 14th 1938 against Germany, in Berlin. Playing before a packed stadium of 100,000 fanatical German supporters. The preparation for this game was not what it should have been. The English team had travelled by train and ferry for many hours. Not good preparation for a game of this magnitude. By comparison the German team were having special training in the Black Forest. The England team also had the humiliation of having to give the Nazi salute. Not one of the England players wanted to do this but Sir Stanley Rouse, the FA Secretary, sought advice from the British Ambassador and it was reluctantly agreed to keep the crowd in a good mood. The England players were now very determined to win this game.

The England team of 1938 reluctantly giving the Nazi salute

The England team that day consisted of: - Woodley; Sproston; Hapgood; Willingham; Young; Welsh; Mathews; Robinson; Broome; Goulden and Bastin.

The pitch was perfect, soft and level. As Cliff Bastin later remarked, young Jackie looked anxious. He was, however, the England star that day. He scored twice and England won 6-3, in one of the most satisfactory performances ever by our national team. After twelve minutes Mathews danced around Muenzenberg and curled in a perfect centre for Goulden to shoot. German goalkeeper Hans Jakob punched it to the feet of Cliff Bastin who made no mistake and England were one up. Not long afterwards the stadium was a sea of red Swastika flags as the Germans equalised. The ecstasy of the stadium was soon cut short by Jackie Robinson taking Cliff Bastin's pass to put England 2-1 up. England were soon 3-1 up courtesy of a Frank Broome goal. Mathews beat four defenders to give England a 4-1 lead. The crowd were stunned. The Germans scored a second through Josef Gauchel to make it 4-2 at half time. Five minutes after the restart, Robinson hit England's fifth. The Germans pulled back through Pesser, but Goulden finished off the Germans with a drive from 25 yards out - so a wonderful victory over the so-called 'Master race'.

The England team won a great victory 6-3.

The second game was on May 21st 1938 against Switzerland at Zurich, before a crowd of 25,000. The England team consisted of: - Woodley; Sproston; Hapgood; Willingham; Young; Welsh; Mathews; Robinson; Broome; Goulden and Bastin. This was the same line up that faced the Germans the week before.

During the run up to the game there was a minimum 30 hours rainfall. The pitch was bumpy, compared with the one they had played on the week before in Berlin.

Robinson played pluckily and dribbled well and indeed from all reports was England's best forward. However they still lost 2-1. After their great victory the week before, this was a most disappointing result. The scorer was Bastin.

The England party outside the Dolder Grand Hotel, Zurich, after beating the Germany 6-3. Jackie is 5th from left.

The day after the Zurich game, Jackie sent a picture postcard of the Dolder Grand Hotel, Zurich to his future mother and father-in-law. It was of a beautiful hotel standing in its own grounds on the outskirts of Zurich.

I think the words on that card sum up the modesty of that young man. Not forgetting that the previous week he had scored 2 goals against the mighty German team, and the day before he had played a blinder against Switzerland, Jackie didn't mention football, he just stated, "I think this hotel is a bit too good for the likes of us."

The third and last match on the tour was against France on the 26th May 1938 at Paris.

The selectors in making sure that everyone got a game rested Jackie for this one.

The team that day was; - Woodley; Sproston; Hapgood; Willingham; Young; Cullis; Broome; Mathews; Drake; Goulden and Bastin.

England won 4-2. The scorers were; - Drake 2, Broome and Bastin.

He went home with added confidence. He knew he could compete and win against the best players in the world. Here was a Shiremoor boy seeing the world, he was still only 20 years and 9 months old.

Now being on the international scene Jackie was invited to the 75th anniversary banquet, held at the Holborn Restaurant, London, on Wednesday 26 October 1938. This was to celebrate the formation of the league (1863-1938). All the celebrities of the day were in attendance.

Young Jackie had arrived.

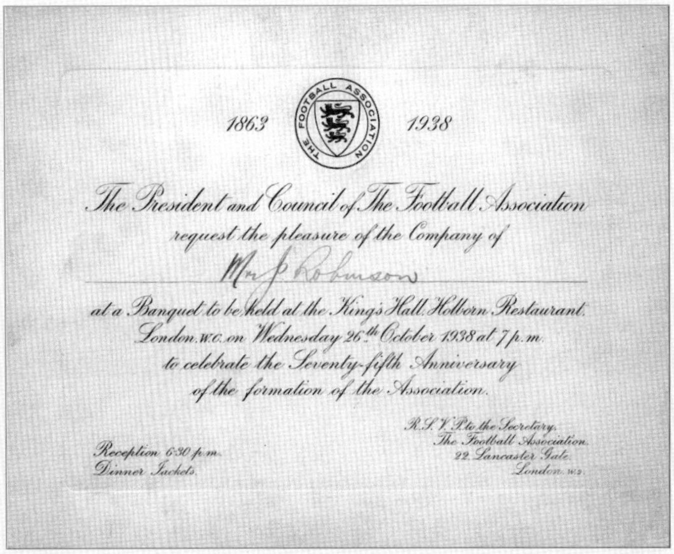

1863 1938

THE FOOTBALL ASSOCIATION

The President and Council of The Football Association
request the pleasure of the Company of
Mr J Robinson
at a Banquet to be held at the King's Hall, Holborn Restaurant,
London, W.C. on Wednesday 26th October 1938 at 7 p.m.
to celebrate the Seventy-fifth Anniversary
of the formation of the Association.

Reception 6.30 p.m.
Dinner Jackets.

R.S.V.P. to the Secretary,
The Football Association,
22, Lancaster Gate,
London. W.2.

Jackie Robinson's Invite to the 75th Anniversary of the formation of the Football Association

Just four days earlier he had played for England against Wales at Cardiff, on October 22nd 1938. The England team that day was; - Woodley; Sproston; Hapgood; Willingham; Young; Copping; Mathews; Robinson; Lawton; Goulden and Boyes. England were beaten 4-2.

The scorers were: - Lawton and Mathews.

Jackie had also been honoured by being selected, a month previous, on 21st September, 1938, to play for the English League against the Irish League in Belfast.

The team was; - Woodley (Chelsea); Sproston (Tottenham Hotspurs); Hapgood (Arsenal); Willingham (Huddersfield Town); Cullis (Wolverhampton Wanderers); Welsh (Charlton Athletic); Mathews (Stoke City); Robinson (Sheffield Wednesday); Lawton (Everton); Goulden (West Ham United); Morton (West Ham United), reserves, Mercer (Everton); Steele (Stoke City).

England won 6-2 and Robinson scored one goal.

The scorers were: - Payne 2, Steele 2, Kirchen, Willingham, Johnson and Robinson.

Due to the war, the next time we saw Jackie in an international shirt was on February 20th 1943 at Glasgow for the England army against the Scotland Army.

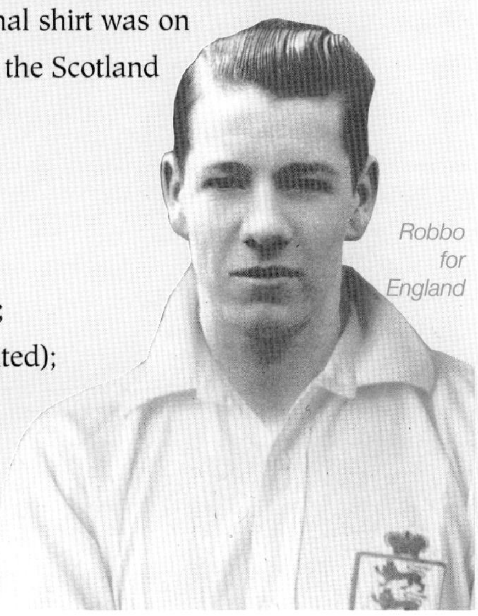

Robbo for England

The England Army team was: - Swift (Manchester City); Bucuzzi (Fulham); Compton L (Arsenal); Britton (Everton); Cullis (Wolverhampton Wanderers); Mercer (Everton); Birkett (Newcastle United); Robinson (Sheffield Wednesday); Westcott (Wolverhampton Wanderers); Hagan (Sheffield United); Compton D (Arsenal).

The result was:

Scottish Army 0 - English Army 7.

The scorers were: - Robinson 4, Westcott 3.

Germany
v
England

Played Saturday 14th May 1938 at the Olympic Stadium Berlin

V. Woodley
(Chelsea)

B. Sproston
(Manchester City)

E. Hapgood
(Arsenal)

K. Willingham
(Huddersfield)

A. Young
(Huddersfield)

D. Welsh
(Charlton Ath)

S. Mathews
(Stoke City)

J Robinson
(Sheffield Wed.)

F. Broome
(Aston Villa)

L. Goulden
(West Ham Un)

C. Bastin
(Arsenal)

England 6; Scorers, Robinson (2), Bastin, Broome, Mathews, Goulden.
Germany 3; Scorers, Gelleach, Gouchel, Peffer.
Attendance; 103,000
The England team pictured in their own club colours.

The England team who beat the Germans 6-3

Chapter Six
Return to Tyneside and Sunderland and F.C.

The 1946-47 season saw Jackie as captain of Sheffield Wednesday, a big honour, but well deserved. In the close season the Wednesday team had travelled to Sweden to play IFK, Malmo, Wednesday won 9-2, another hat trick for Jackie.

Six goals in the first seven games was Jackie's way of signing off for the club he had joined when he was 16 years of age. The Wednesday directors came to the conclusion that it might be both in their interests and in Jackie Robinson's to place him on the transfer list.

He had been training at Newcastle and it is not the best policy for the club captain to be away from the other players all week. West Bromwich Albion had been trying to secure his services for some time. Albion obviously remembered the amazing circumstances in which Jackie had made his entry into big time football. He had played against them the week before the F.A cup final in 1935. That day he had played like a seasoned veteran. He had ball control and a body swerve almost unbelievable in a youngster, and what is more he scored against them. In fact, this was the first time that even some of the Wednesday first team players had seen him.

Jackie seen here signing for Sunderland FC with Willie Murray the Black Cats Manager

However it was not to be, Mr E. W. Taylor, the Wednesday manager, stated that Robinson did not wish to join a Southern or Midlands club, he wanted to join a Northern club, and Sunderland being local for Jackie, were keen to sign him. So that is where he was to go. A record fee for Wednesday of £7,000 had been paid by Aston Villa for Starling. It was assumed £8,000 would be involved for Jackie.

Wednesday had circulated clubs that Jackie Robinson, their captain and international inside right was available for transfer. They believed his age was 27. This was October 1946.

Willie Murray, the astute Sunderland manager, who was bidding for Robinson, discovered through his army record papers, that Robinson was in fact 29. Then Robinson called at Roker Park, manager Murray asked him point blank 'how old are you Jack?' the Sheffield man replied, "29".

Murray had offered £8.000 and the offer had been accepted, . He promptly cut his offer, the difference of those two years represented to him, two fifths off the price and the fee was adjusted. Preston North End then came on the scene, but Robinson left with the final choice, chose the wearsiders. A contributing factor was that during the war he partnered Whitelum, Sunderland's centre forward in a regimental eleven, and got on well with him.

Jackie seen here sitting next to Cliff Whitelum who he later played with at Sunderland

They had also played on the same side in a charity match for Billy Forrest's team against George Camsell's team, on 5th May 1943 at Ayresome Park, Middlesbrough.

Jackie was stationed at Middlesbrough for a while with the army.

Eric Taylor the secretary/manager of Sheffield Wednesday had written to Jackie a few days after he had scored the only Sheffield goal in the 1-1 draw against Bradford on the 13th March 1943, thanking him for 'knocking the usual one in'. He had also mentioned that he had seen the directors about having C.W of Sunderland in the team to play against Nottingham on Saturday 20th March 1943, but that they were sticking by the same team. It was not unusual for guest players to be included in the war years.

This letter shows Jackie's loyalty to his friend Cliff Whitelum. It also reveals the influence he was beginning to have in helping with suggestions for the Sheffield team. It would have helped

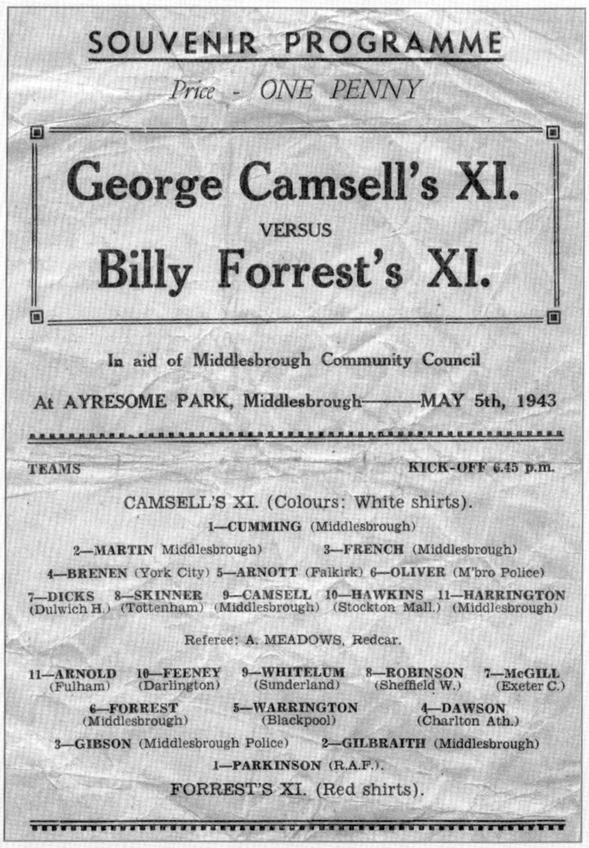

SOUVENIR PROGRAMME

Price - ONE PENNY

George Camsell's XI.

VERSUS

Billy Forrest's XI.

In aid of Middlesbrough Community Council

At AYRESOME PARK, Middlesbrough——MAY 5th, 1943

TEAMS KICK-OFF 6.45 p.m.

CAMSELL'S XI. (Colours: White shirts).

1—CUMMING (Middlesbrough)

2—MARTIN Middlesbrough) 3—FRENCH (Middlesbrough)

4—BRENEN (York City) 5—ARNOTT (Falkirk) 6—OLIVER (M'bro Police)

7—DICKS (Dulwich H.) 8—SKINNER (Tottenham) 9—CAMSELL (Middlesbrough) 10—HAWKINS (Stockton Mall.) 11—HARRINGTON (Middlesbrough)

Referee: A. MEADOWS, Redcar.

11—ARNOLD (Fulham) 10—FEENEY (Darlington) 9—WHITELUM (Sunderland) 8—ROBINSON (Sheffield W.) 7—McGILL (Exeter C.)

6—FORREST (Middlesbrough) 5—WARRINGTON (Blackpool) 4—DAWSON (Charlton Ath.)

3—GIBSON (Middlesbrough Police) 2—GILBRAITH (Middlesbrough)

1—PARKINSON (R.A.F.).

FORREST'S XI. (Red shirts).

Robinson, Sheffield Wednesday and Cliff Whitelum, Sunderland playing together in the Billy Forrest XI.

that this was the season when he had just scored six hat tricks and had played for the England army against the Scotland army.

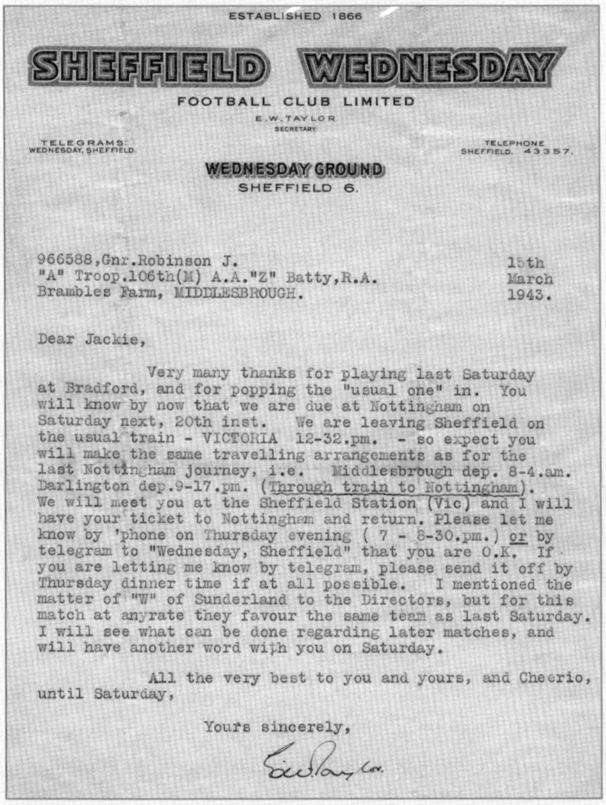

ESTABLISHED 1866

SHEFFIELD WEDNESDAY

FOOTBALL CLUB LIMITED

E.W.TAYLOR
SECRETARY

TELEGRAMS:
WEDNESDAY, SHEFFIELD.

TELEPHONE
SHEFFIELD. 43357.

WEDNESDAY GROUND
SHEFFIELD 6.

966588,Gnr.Robinson J.
"A" Troop.106th(M) A.A."Z" Batty,R.A.
Brambles Farm, MIDDLESBROUGH.

15th
March
1943.

Dear Jackie,

Very many thanks for playing last Saturday at Bradford, and for popping the "usual one" in. You will know by now that we are due at Nottingham on Saturday next, 20th inst. We are leaving Sheffield on the usual train - VICTORIA 12-32.pm. - so expect you will make the same travelling arrangements as for the last Nottingham journey, i.e. Middlesbrough dep. 8-4.am. Darlington dep.9-17.pm. (Through train to Nottingham). We will meet you at the Sheffield Station (Vic) and I will have your ticket to Nottingham and return. Please let me know by 'phone on Thursday evening (7 - 8-30.pm.) or by telegram to "Wednesday, Sheffield" that you are O.K. If you are letting me know by telegram, please send it off by Thursday dinner time if at all possible. I mentioned the matter of "W" of Sunderland to the Directors, but for this match at anyrate they favour the same team as last Saturday. I will see what can be done regarding later matches, and will have another word with you on Saturday.

All the very best to you and yours, and Cheerio, until Saturday,

Yours sincerely,

The letter from Sheffield Wednesday secretary Eric Taylor during the war.

The days at Sunderland were happy for Jackie. He was playing before crowds of 40.000 regularly for home games. In his three seasons with them he scored 32 league goals plus 2 F.A cup goals.

The social life was good at Sunderland, he played golf with all his team mates. The team did rounds of the pubs and clubs promoting the club's image, and doing work for charities, and supporting people less able than themselves. There is in my possession a photograph of the Sunderland team signing a ball at the Wheatcheaf in Benton Square near Whitley bay. This was Jackie's local public house. 'Just William' was being performed at the Sunderland Empire and several of the cast, including William and Violet Elizabeth Bott came up to meet the players in training.

The show business side was not unusual for Jackie. While with Sheffield he had attended many of the big London productions as guests of the London football clubs. He also had a great friend who was in show business, Pat Healy. There is a link between Jackie, Pat and myself which I will pursue in a later chapter.

Seasons 1946-47 to 1948-49 saw Jackie Robinson happily back in his beloved Tyneside. At Sheffield Wednesday he had been idolised. Although there was not quite that frenzy at Sunderland, he entertained the crowd with some brilliant displays. Team mates Len Shackleton and Barney Ramsden ,the ex-Liverpool player who played half back just behind Jackie, had many kind comments to make to Mrs Robinson after Jackie's death.

The young cast of Just William, playing at the Local Theatre meet the Sunderland players, Whitelum, Robinson and Hall

There were a lot of prima donnas arriving now on the football scene who wanted all they could get out of football. Playing from 18 to 32 on average with just 14 years to impress and make money which had to last them for life. Retirement was usually to a public house, this seemed the favourite job.

When playing for Sheffield Wednesday, Jackie was living in a lovely house in a very respectable area of the city. While in Sunderland he was in an ordinary house in Shiremoor, far below the standard of what he had left in Sheffield. He was philosophical enough to say 'it will have to do until something better comes along' certainly not the words of a big head. Fame had not affected his judgement. Here was a shy humble man, a big man.

A sport cartoon from the Newcastle Evening Chronicle of January 1947. The cartoon is indicating Jackie scoring four goals against Blackpool.

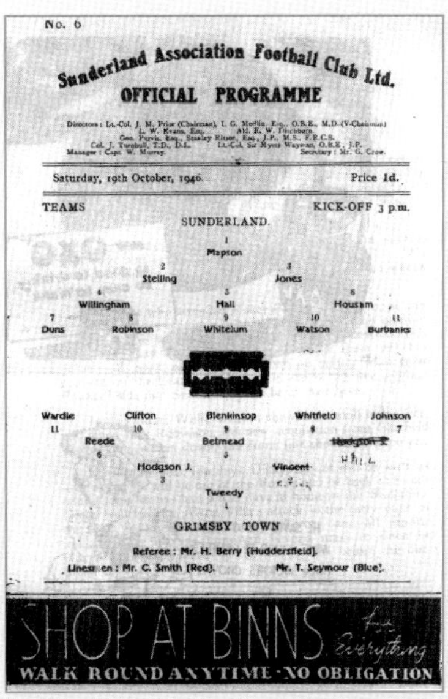

No. 6

Sunderland Association Football Club Ltd.

OFFICIAL PROGRAMME

Saturday, 19th October, 1946. Price 1d.

TEAMS KICK-OFF 3 p.m.

SUNDERLAND.

1 Mapson

2 Stelling 3 Jones

4 Willingham 5 Hall 6 Housam

7 Duns 8 Robinson 9 Whitelum 10 Watson 11 Burbanks

Wardie 11 Clifton 10 Blenkinsop 9 Whitfield 8 Johnson 7

Reede 6 Betmead 5 Hodgson E.

Hodgson J. 3 Vincent

Tweedy 1

GRIMSBY TOWN

Referee: Mr. H. Berry (Huddersfield).

Linesmen: Mr. C. Smith (Red). Mr. T. Seymour (Blue).

SHOP AT BINNS for Everything

WALK ROUND ANYTIME - NO OBLIGATION

Jackie Robinson's first game for Sunderland on 19th October, 1946 against Grimsby Town.

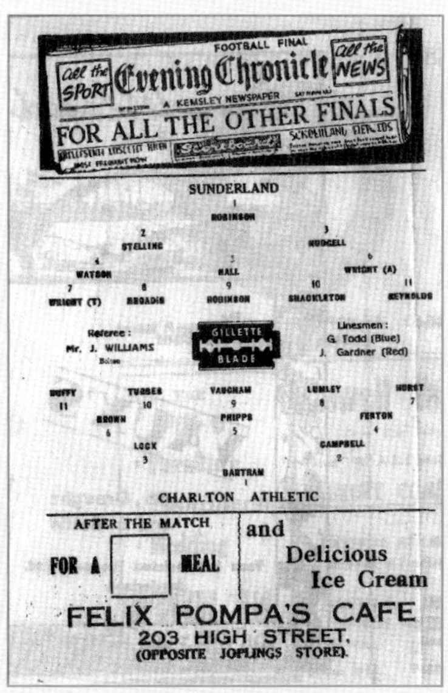

FOOTBALL FINAL

All the SPORT Evening Chronicle All the NEWS

A KEMSLEY NEWSPAPER

FOR ALL THE OTHER FINALS

SUNDERLAND

1 ROBINSON

2 STELLING 3 HUDGELL

4 WATSON 5 HALL 6 WRIGHT (A)

7 WRIGHT (T) 8 BROADIS 9 ROBINSON 10 SHACKLETON 11 REYNOLDS

Referee: Mr. J. WILLIAMS Bolton

GILLETTE BLADE

Linesmen: G. Todd (Blue) J. Gardner (Red)

DUFFY 11 TURNER 10 VAUGHAN 9 LUMLEY 8 HURST 7

BROWN 6 PHIPPS 5 FENTON 4

LOCK 3 CAMPBELL 2

BARTRAM 1

CHARLTON ATHLETIC

AFTER THE MATCH FOR A MEAL and Delicious Ice Cream

FELIX POMPA'S CAFE

203 HIGH STREET.

(OPPOSITE JOPLINGS STORE).

Jackie Robinson's last game for Sunderland on 23rd April, 1949 against Charlton Athletic

A caricature of Jackie in his Sunderland Days

Jackie in various team photographs with his Sunderland team mates from 1946-1949

Chapter Seven
Lincoln City F.C Player/Coach

At the age of 32 Jackie went to Lincoln City as their player-coach. This was to be a new challenge for him. He had much to give to the up and coming young footballers.
It was no surprise that he was wanted by Lincoln. In his first game they won 3 – 0 and Jackie had scored one of the best goals ever seen on that ground.
So 1949 was to be the start of a new career as coach. He would eventually cease to play, and be the coach full time. In theory this was what Jackie hoped would happen.
Lincoln were in the third division, Jackie was an international player. All the hard men were after his scalp and he wasn't going to make them look foolish. Week after week, he dazzled, and then in his ninth game for the club, disaster struck. His leg was broken in a fall, and this complicated fracture saw the end of his career as a player, and sadly also as a coach. The many offers of condolence were no help to Jackie who was heartbroken in hospital for many weeks. He lost interest in the sport to which he had given his all: a schoolboy county player at 13, an England international player at 19, wonderful service to Sheffield Wednesday, Sunderland, and indeed in the short space of time to Lincoln. He was devastated. However, this situation did not last.
As all who knew him realised Jackie, was a fighter.

Jackie Robinson, ex-Sunderland footballer, now with Lincoln, takes a look at the outsize wooden spoon presented to Backworth Hotel, who finished at the bottom of the local darts league last

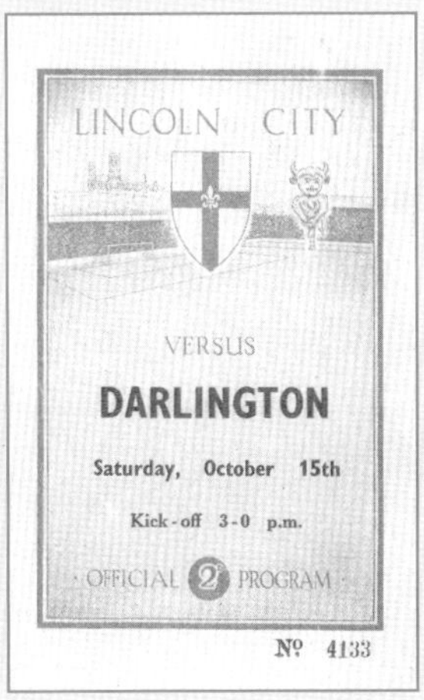

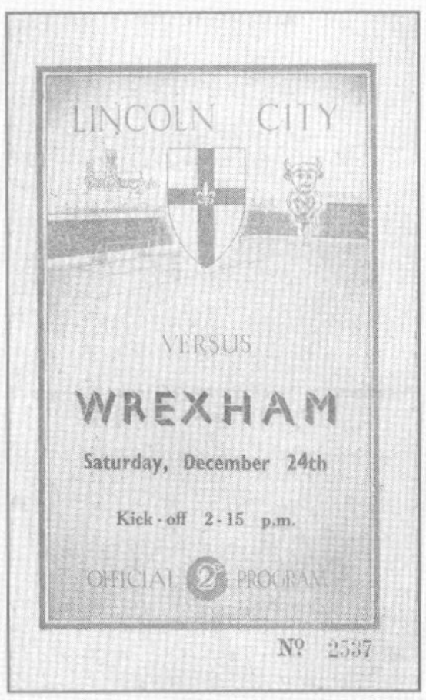

Above: Jackie at the Lincoln pub, The Backworth Hotel, presenting the wooden spoon.

left: The programmes of Jackie's first and last games for Lincoln City.

The two programmes depicted are supplied by Don Natterstad a Lincoln City historian.

Chapter Eight

Jackie the family man

Above: Lillian on a nostalgic trip back to Hillsborough, the arena where Jackie Robinson was the hero of Sheffield Wednesday.

In dealing with Jackie the family man, I am also going to include his relationship with his friends.

I did remark in an earlier chapter about Jackie and Lillian becoming a lifelong romance.

Jackie was the school hero. He was a champion runner, a good rugby player and a county footballer. Everyone liked to be seen with him, he was very popular.

Lillian was a bright scholar and very pretty, she was not without her admirers. She had two brothers Billy and Eric Casson. They knew and got on well with Jackie. This was a good starting point for a schoolgirl/schoolboy romance. Jackie was fifteen, Lillian was only twelve and a quarter, and their young lives were happy. They went their own separate ways of course. At that age, and with their strict upbringing, it was expected.

When Jackie was signed up by Sheffield Wednesday, everyone in the village was proud, but none more so than Lillian. Of course there was a feeling of apprehension. Would Jackie forget her, would he find some other girl down in Sheffield? She need have had no worries, there was only one girl in the world for him; Lillian Casson was that girl.

After he had played against West Bromwich Albion at the age of 17 years and 8 months, and went with the victorious Sheffield Wednesday side to Wembley, he returned home to Shiremoor for the close season. Everyone wanted to shake his hand, he was indeed a local boy made good, and Lillian was just fifteen.

In those days of the steam train the journeys from Newcastle to Sheffield were long and monotonous, but the thoughts that soon he would be seeing his Lillian seemed to make the train go faster. When they were together he thought the journey had all been worthwhile. Of course he kept in touch with his beloved Lillian. In 1937 Jackie was already establishing himself in the Wednesday team, and he was chosen to play for England against Finland at Helsinki. Jackie used to talk to Lillian about his travels throughout the country, and now throughout the world, but reluctantly. He was a very unassuming young gentleman. There were no airs and graces about him whatsoever.

By the end of the 1937-38 season he was chosen to go on the Continental Tour with England to Germany, Switzerland and France. Before going on this tour he and Lillian had been thinking of marriage. After a wonderful tour, he came home, told his landlady in Sheffield he would be wanting a bigger room, and advanced with all haste to Shiremoor to see Lillian and her parents. He had sent a card to Mr and Mrs Casson from Switzerland with a photograph of the Dolder Grand Hotel, Zurich. The beautiful hotel is were the England team stayed on tour.

On the 12th of October 1938, on a Wednesday, appropriately, Jackie and Lillian were married at Killingworth parish church, near Whitley Bay.

They had tried to make it a quiet wedding, but the papers got wind of it, and their photographs were shown all over the country.

At last they were together, Jackie was 21 years and 2 months, Lillian was 18 years and 5 months. The previous Saturday, Jackie had scored a goal in Wednesday's win over Manchester City.

That Saturday he would travel with the team to Southampton. Lillian stayed in the digs. She was very happy and she used to prepare the meals for Jackie for when he got home from training. Several of the Sheffield Wednesday players were also staying at the same lodgings, and they had a fine time together, they used to play tricks on Lillian like putting pebbles in the bed or tying the sheets together. When Lillian was expecting a child they moved into a lovely semi-detached house in an elevated position overlooking the city.

Jackie wanted the best for his child and after training his time was taken up preparing the nursery. He got a list of private nursing homes, and Lillian chose one called 'The Drive', not far from her house in Sheffield.

On 16th April, arriving early came Yvonne, it must have been pure intuition on the part of Lillian and Jackie to pick that name, because it fits in very well for her, this French sounding name, with the French surname she was to acquire later in life.

She was a tiny baby, and quite poorly for a while. However, with all the attention this devoted couple lavished upon her, she quickly got well. 1939 saw the start of World War Two, Sheffield was a dangerous city for a mother and young daughter to live in, with Germans bombing the city, Jackie joined the army and Lillian and their daughter Yvonne moved back to the north-east.

War is a terrible thing and Lillian was to lose her brother Billy who was killed in action at sea. This was a tragic time. Jackie got on with his duties in the forces, and when time allowed, he played for Sheffield Wednesday.

A very determined looking, young, Jackie Robinson

In fact during the war years Jackie scored 91 goals out of 109 games, a remarkable record.

1946-49 saw Jackie move to Sunderland F.C. This was a lot easier for his family. He had been offered terms with clubs in the Midlands, down south and Preston, but his roots were in the northeast.

Yvonne was now seven and settled in school. Lillian was among family and friends, Jackie was home, everything was beginning to become real again, after that terrible war.

In 1949 an offer came for Jackie to be coach-player with Lincoln City, this was not to be turned down. As a coach Jackie could extend his life in football. He talked it over with Lillian and found he would have to travel to and from Lincoln. This meant Yvonne need not be disturbed from her schooling.

Lillian wouldn't need to uproot her home, and go off to meet new friends just yet.

They would try for a season to see how it was going, and then maybe they would all move to Lincoln.

Fate had other things planned for Jackie and his family. After only nine games Lillian had to go down to Lincoln. Jackie was in hospital with complicated fractures of his leg, and sadly he was never to play competitive football again.

It is said that behind every good man there is a good lady. This was certainly the case regarding Lillian. Jackie was really down in the dumps, his career shattered by an accident which was going to change his life style.

Lillian was about two months pregnant with their second child and said, "Come on Jackie there is another world after football, let's get on with it." On May 19th 1950 daughter Jacqueline was born. Two years later on July 3rd 1952 son Raymond was born.

So here was Jackie coming up to 35, with an adoring wife, two daughters and a son, what work was he going to do?

Jackie had a great friend in Shiremoor; an Irishman from Galway called Pat Healy. Pat could talk the hind leg off a donkey. He was still a charming man and a real gentleman. He was in show business, a beautiful Irish tenor singer and he was also a professional artist. He came over to England, met his wife Mary, who was a nurse, and settled in the northeast. He has been on almost every theatre in the British Isles. At one time he was understudy to Joseph Locke, the great Irish tenor.

Pat was impeccably dressed and the women used to flock round him. Lillian used to like Jackie going out with Pat. With Jackie being so shy, and Pat being so outgoing and extrovert, she thought it was good for Jackie to be brought out of his shell.

They were to be good mates. When show business suffered a decline, Pat decided he would try to open a barbers shop to help Mary and their small family. With no hesitation Jackie loaned Pat the money to set up his shop. Eric, Lillian's brother, who was a joiner, made Pat a barber's pole. Pat never forgot his kindness, and talks about it to this day.

Jackie said to Pat "You are a famous sportsman, what do other sportsmen do when they retire?"

"They get a pub that's what they do".

Lillian and Jackie talked about Pat's suggestion. If a bloke like Pat Healy thought Jackie could do it; well it was certainly worth a try.

Pat had told him that the breweries would be fighting each other to get him and of course Pat was right.

Chapter Nine

Life After Soccer

"Jackie Robinson after a pub". It was the talk of the terraces at St. James Park, Newcastle. After all just because he was worshiped as a god down Sheffield Wednesday didn't mean that the locals of Newcastle and the surrounding area, didn't think well of him. He was after all a local boy that they were proud of. He had played for West Wylam a local junior team. "Well when he gets it, we'll be there," they exclaimed.

Jackie was offered "The Ship" at Gateshead. It was a success. The fans flocked to it. Newcastle United and Sunderland players used to drop in for a chat with Jackie.

Jackie was a fair dart thrower and he organised teams in the local dart league. When he was at Sheffield he had regularly played in charity games. This was an ideal opportunity for his public house with him at the helm, to help other people.

This was the kind of person he was and he would help anyone. Speaking of Jackie's interests in darts it has certainly rubbed off on his son Raymond. Raymond has played for the county at darts, he is presently the county team manager, and he has been on Jim Bowen's "Bullseye" programme on the television.

His father would have been proud of him. Daughter Yvonne is also a fair darts player, and just recently won a championship competition at Carlisle. Her two daughters, Jackie's grand daughters, are also into darts and play in the local league. Both Dawn and Heather have won trophies whilst playing the sport. Daughter Jacqueline can also play a bit. Pat Healy, who is the kind of person that other singers like to follow, would go along to "The Ship" and many a good singing night would be held there.

However, Lillian was bringing up three children, Jacqueline and Raymond were still very young, so it was hard work. Jackie was having problems with his leg although he never complained.

They decided after much thought to terminate their employment with the brewery. The brewery tried to persuade them to change their minds but to no avail. The pub was doing very well; they would miss the charming couple. But whatever will be, will be.

They moved back to Shiremoor, Jackie played in a few charity matches but was told by the doctor, any more games, and he would be a permanent cripple.

Every year at Shiremoor they have what they call 'The Treat'. The local community save throughout the year, and on the first Saturday in July the children march to a huge field, the treat field and sweets and pop are handed out to every child. This is a tradition that has been going for years. Jackie used to volunteer his services to referee the football matches for the school children and juniors.

He showed certain strictness towards his children, however he never raised a hand, he only had to raise his voice, and his wish would be obeyed. Home life was very happy indeed, Lillian was pleased, knowing the active sporting life that her husband had been used to, she thought he might be unsettled after football. Obviously he was at times, but it was nothing she couldn't handle.

There were a lot of hangers on, but she could tell the genuine ones, and soon put Jackie right on that score. He was soft hearted, and an easy touch for a sob story. Lillian was a wise lady.

The children were growing up and in 1957 daughter Yvonne got married, she was eighteen, he was very proud of her and said she looked beautiful.

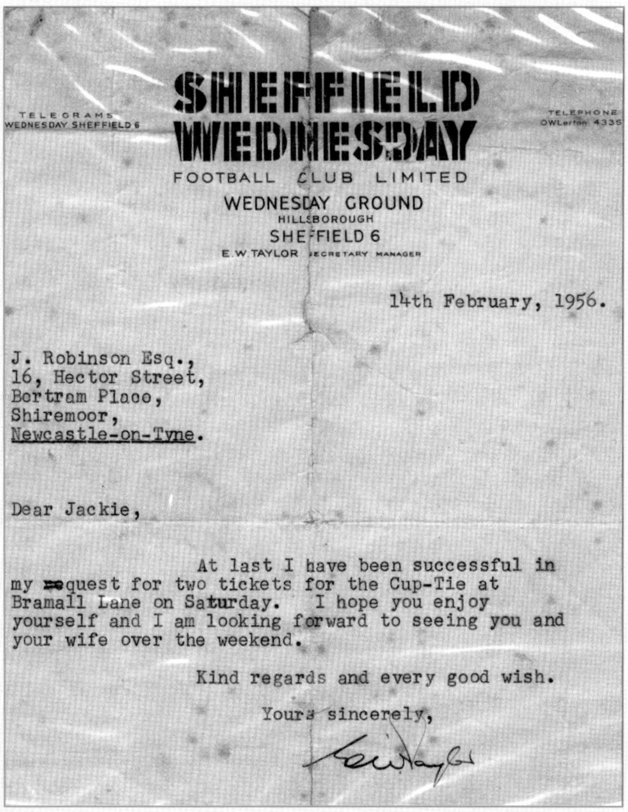

TELEGRAMS WEDNESDAY SHEFFIELD 6

SHEFFIELD WEDNESDAY

TELEPHONE OWLerton 4335

FOOTBALL CLUB LIMITED
WEDNESDAY GROUND
HILLSBOROUGH
SHEFFIELD 6
E. W. TAYLOR SECRETARY MANAGER

14th February, 1956.

J. Robinson Esq.,
16, Hector Street,
Bertram Place,
Shiremoor,
Newcastle-on-Tyne.

Dear Jackie,

At last I have been successful in my request for two tickets for the Cup-Tie at Bramall Lane on Saturday. I hope you enjoy yourself and I am looking forward to seeing you and your wife over the weekend.

Kind regards and every good wish.

Yours sincerely,

E W Taylor

left:
A letter to Jackie from Eric Taylor

Chapter Ten

The Final Years.

In writing this chapter to Jackie's life it is not a sad occasion; rather it is a triumphant waking of all the pleasure he gave.

Jackie did suffer it is true; he had so much pain towards the end. He didn't give up easily when he was recovering after having 2 strokes and kidney problems, Jackie and a friend he made in hospital Ray Tennick decided to raise funds for the hospital. Ray was a cashier with the North Shields F.C. They organised a football match and lots of the Newcastle, Sunderland and Sheffield players turned out, including the great Jackie Milburn. Jackie was not just thinking about himself. The doctors and nursing staff had been marvellous with him and he wanted to do something for them and their patients in return.

Jackie was in a wheelchair for the later years of his life, and only Lillian was allowed to push him. This she did willingly. He died of cancer in July 1972.

Throughout these years of illness, money was scarce but Jackie just got on with it. His friends helped whenever they could. Charlie Crowe the ex-Newcastle United player who was now in the 'North Star Hotel', Longbenton, organised a charity evening and Sheffield Wednesday F. C sent an autographed football which was auctioned and fetched £30.00. This was in 1970.

There is a photograph in my keeping of Jackie and one of his Wednesday teammates in 1939 getting sunray tonic. Indeed this special man was a tonic to everyone he came in contact with. He had no enemies, but lots and lots of friends.

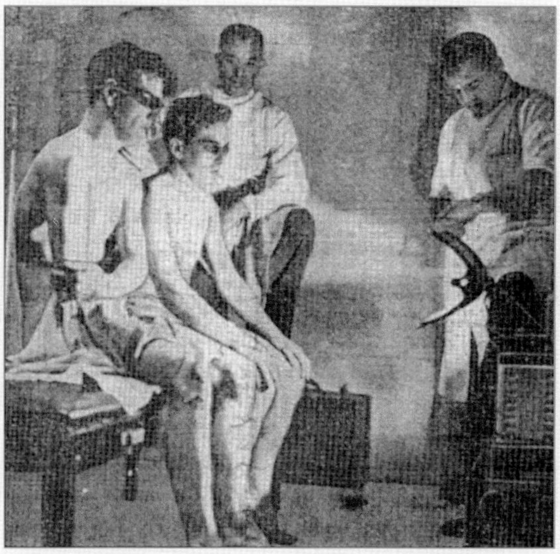

A sun ray tonic for Robinson and Thompson, two Sheffield Wednesday stalwarts, who are watched by trainer Powell (left) and his assistant, Swain.

Jackie had pen pals who worshiped him. Jackie answered as many as he could, but he was a very busy young gentleman. Lillian even used to reply to some fans for him. One prince from the now defunct Gold Coast in Africa even wrote to him. This is very fitting for a true prince of football. – Jackie Robinson.

Chapter Eleven

Change of mind

Although it was my intention to only write eleven chapters I am sure you will agree every good team needs a good reserve. I think you will enjoy this additional chapter.

My wife Yvonne and I on our travels to Portugal and Malta have met several football supporters who saw Jackie play. In one conversation with a group of Sheffield United supporters I was told that he had scored one of the best goals ever seen at Bramall Lane, praise indeed from a rival supporter.

Another supporter told me how when he was little he used to live around the corner from Jackie's digs; Jackie would play football in the street with him. When the boy told his father, he said, "well son you've played with the best there is"

One important meeting I had in Malta was with a Norwegian free-lance football correspondent named Kare M Torgimsen. He was covering the Malta v Norway football match. We chatted and got on really well. He told me about how Graham Taylor had spent an hour giving an interview to the Norwegian press. He was impressed with Graham and so am I; he was very harshly treated by our press. Just look at his record, I would have been proud of it.

Kare and I have been in touch by post on a regular basis and he has helped me with advice and by sending me statistics and articles from Germany, Switzerland and England.

Since starting this book I have been thrilled to see a video of Jackie playing against Germany in Berlin, and saw his two goals. It was a fantastic moment for me.

For my mother-in-law, Mrs Lillian Robinson's' 74th birthday on the 24th April 1994 we gave her an unexpected surprise by taking her to Hillsborough, at the kind invitation of the Sheffield Wednesday club. I informed the 'Sheffield Star' newspaper we would be there at a certain time and if there were any of Jackie's fans we would be delighted to see them. What a wonderful day it was my mother-in-law Lillian, my wife Yvonne, my sister-in-law Jacqueline and I, arrived by car and were immediately surrounded by about twenty supporters. I realised what a special person my father-in-law had been to create this interest after all those years.

It had been 1946 when Jackie left for Sunderland F.C yet here 48 years later his fans were lining up to talk to his wife and daughters.

We looked at the trophies won by the club, chatted to members of staff including manager Trevor Francis and player Chris Waddle, the England international. The fans all had their special reflections on Jackie's career and showed interest in my proposed book. Many of them had their own scrapbooks.

We took phone numbers, names and addresses and have kept in touch. In one such phone conversation I was told of a fan that idolised Jackie and was always talking about him. His young grandson on hearing of Jackie's death in 1972 said to his grandfather: "Never mind grandad, when you die you will go to heaven and meet Jackie Robinson".

I wrote to Sir Stanley Matthews and he replied with a very nice letter in which he said Jackie was a very fine player indeed.

I had written to Lincoln City but they had no old records, so knowing that Graham Taylor had once been their manager, I wrote to him at Wolverhampton Wanderers F.C Graham was most interested in Jackie's part in England's victory over the Germans in 1938. He invited my wife and I to be his guests at Molineux.

It will be nice to finish with some acknowledgments from various football publications.

"Graceful, eye-catching inside right of much talent. Could dribble, shoot and pass well, was a schemer and always willing to assist his defence".

"Inside right a major discovery of the thirties, a much talented, graceful prodigy". A writer of the times tells of "Jackie's brilliant natural talents as a boy and that in the development of his play he has always shown remarkable and exceptional ease and certainty in his ball control" he was a Wednesday regular long before his 20th birthday.

Jackie Robinson has been described as one of the greatest inside forwards in Wednesday's history. He had everything, superb ball control a tremendous burst of speed, body swerve and a remarkable talent for scoring goals. How much more the man from Shiremoor might have achieved but for the war. Yet ironically, it is for his feats in the war years that he is probably best remembered. In that period he scored 91 goals in 109 outings with his 35 in 1942/43 including six hat tricks, Robinson was given his first taste of league soccer in 1935 and within weeks of gaining a regular place in 1936 was playing in an international trial. He gained the first of his four England caps in May 1937 against Finland, naturally he scored. Robinson was touching a peak in that 1938/39 campaign when the Owls so nearly gained promotion, but, if the war halted his progress, it did so only temporarily. In 1942/43 when Wednesday enjoyed their best wartime season, Robinson turned in some of his best performances and incidentally, some colleagues insisted that he was never better than when he had sunk a few pints before the game.

Note:

In 1946/47 as Sheffield Wednesday captain, Jackie scored 6 goals in 7 games. He went on to Sunderland and scored another 18 goals in 31 games, so 24 goals from 38 games. Not bad for a man who's star was thought to be fading.

I hope you liked the story of Jackie Robinson and agree with me that this quiet, shy, unassuming young man was a hero to the people who knew him, the people of Shiremoor, his family and his friends.

Jackie Robinson, right, in goalscoring form for Sheffield Wednesday

Chapter Twelve
The Quest, who to approach?

Alan and his friend David were over to do a couple of gigs for Pat Healy. Alan was a country and western singer and David was a tenor singer. David was a Geordie and had known Pat for years, they kept in touch and Pat had booked the pair of them for a concert.

One of their friends, a singer form the Northeast invited them to one of the local pubs, they went along and while they were there Alan spotted two beautiful ladies enter the room, one was a blonde, one had jet-black hair. He looked over, but didn't approach them in case they were spoken for.

Two months later Alan and David were up on another booking, and visited the same pub, once again the ladies came in. They sat at the table with a friend whom they had met on their travels. He was Eric Casson.

The ladies were Lillian Robinson who was the blonde and her daughter Yvonne who was the dark haired one. This time they spoke and indeed Yvonne took Alan's Stetson and put it on her head. He kissed both the ladies good night and got Yvonne's telephone number.

They phoned each other regularly and arranged to meet at York. Yvonne had been through two unhappy marriages, Alan had lost his second wife through illness and he had been divorced once. They instantly hit it off and saw each other whenever they could, eventually getting married one year later, at York.

Yvonne said she was born in Sheffield, and her father had been a famous international footballer, named Jackie Robinson. Alan was very interested as he had played Rugby Union himself until he was 39.

Yvonne and Alan were visiting friends in Liverpool and they all decided to go around the new shopping centre in the dockland area. They came across a shop selling cigarette cards. "There are a lot of footballers over here Yvonne", said Alan, "let's see if your dad is there". Sure enough they spotted him, in the blue and white of Sheffield Wednesday. They asked the man to make a frame with ten famous footballers on, including Jackie; and got one for Lillian also.

Yvonne was absolutely thrilled. She had no photos of her dad, since brother Raymond had been given his cards, photos and other memorabilia.

Alan then decided to take Yvonne to Sheffield, her home town. She was of course a real Geordie now, but they had found where her mum and dad lived, where she was born, and even a couple of the pubs her dad had drunk in.

There was an old gentleman in one of the pubs who remembered Jackie very well, and said he was idolised down in Sheffield.

Yvonne and Alan took Lillian to the Lake District one day, and by chance they had a meal in a lovely country house "The Hare and Hound" at Bowlands bridge. It was owned by Peter Thompson, the ex-Liverpool, Preston N.E and England international footballer, he had a trophy case, filled with his caps and medals. They had a wonderful evening talking about his father-in-law, and Peter offered advice.

Lillian could see by now that Alan was serious in trying to find out more about her beloved Jackie. Even though he had died on July 30th 1972 just before his 55th birthday, she had never stopped loving him, and never re-married. She still is a beautiful lady and has had many admirers, but there is only one man for her, Jackie Robinson, she has many happy memories.

She said she would ask son Raymond for the newspaper cuttings and the scrapbooks. Raymond dutifully obliged. Alan started to collect all the information, which was scattered in various bags, and catalogued them, and put them into albums.

Alan wrote to Sheffield Wednesday, Sunderland and Lincoln City, all previous clubs where Jackie had played. Norma Lane, secretary to the manager at Sheffield Wednesday was very helpful and sent photographs and literature. More information was obtained by going through the sports section in the local library and taking photocopies. Lancaster Gate the address of the football association in London replied, but did not give much information, the Sheffield Star was exceedingly helpful and sent as much about Jackie as it could.

Newcastle United from whom he had guested in 1941 also kindly replied. A few weeks previously they had put an article in their programme about Jackie saying he had been a local boy made good with Sheffield Wednesday.

I am Alan you probably have guessed, I would become Jackie's son-in-law.

Barnie Ramsden the ex-Liverpool, Sunderland player wrote a lovely letter to my mother-in-law when Jackie died. She has kept it all these 21 years. She has also kept her love for Jackie; I told you this was a great romance, sixty years of undying love.

That's my mother-in-law for you, a beautiful, kind lady who wouldn't hurt a fly.

The work I have done in writing this book has led me to believe that we would have got on well together, Jackie and I. We had and have that passion for sport.

The reason for writing eleven chapters towards Jackie's story is the fact that he was a team man. A team of eleven players warrants no less than eleven chapters of that fine player's life.

Jackie Robinson

J. ROBINSON

JACKIE
ROBINSON
Sheffield W

UNFORGETTABLES
JACKIE
ROBINSON

Caricature of Wednesday's
Jackie Robinson by Head

The first match Jackie Robinson played for Sheffield Wednesday was away at the Hawthorns versus West Bromwich Albion.

The Germany v England programme 1938 - Jackie Robinson scored 2 goals in this game.

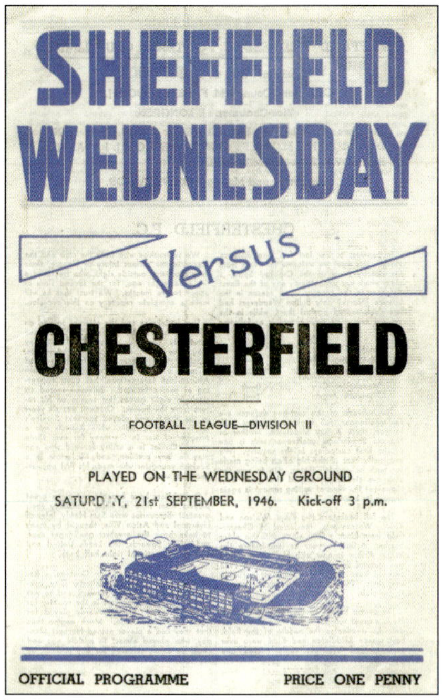

Sheffield Wednesday against Chesterfield - Jackie's last game for the Owls

Sheffield United programme in 1945 when they were playing Sheffield Wednesday.

Sheffield Wednesday against Sunderland

Sheffield Wednesday versus Sheffield United in the 1945 County Cup Final which Wednesday won 4-2

Some programmes from the career of Jackie Robinson
First league game against WBA in 1935, he scored in a 1-1 draw;
Germany v England international, he scored two goals in a 6-3 victory;
Last game for Sheffield Wednesday against Chesterfield in 1946;
Wednesdays first league game against United, after the war;
Versus his home team of Sunderland in 1945;
The County Cup Final which the Owls won 4-2, and once again Jackie scored.

Sheffield Wednesday 1939

Back row left to right:

Millership, Hanford, Ashley, Goodfellow, Catlin, Burrows, ?

Middle row left to right:

? Robinson, Hunt, Napier, Fallon

Front row left to right:

Russell, Lowes

8th MAY, 1943. PRICE TWOPENCE.

Football League (War) Cup

FINAL.

SHEFFIELD WEDNESDAY GROUND,

SATURDAY, 8th MAY, 1943.

KICK-OFF 3.15 p.m.

SHEFFIELD WEDNESDAY

VERSUS

BLACKPOOL

Official Programme.

Sheffield Wednesday - 1943 Wartime Cup final second leg at Hillsborough

Back row l-r: Eric Taylor, Russell, Ashley, Millership, Morton, Gadsby, Cockcroft, Catlin. Middle row l-r: Reynolds, Robinson, Melling, Thompson, Swift, Powell Trainer. Hillsborough. Note the vast crowd (a wartime cup final record). On the right the Cup final programme.

NB Ted Catlin who played in the first leg of the cup final against Blackpool, which ended 2-2, can be seen standing on right of picture sporting a walking stick. He broke his leg in the first game at Blackpool.

Sheffield Wednesday 1946

Back row left to right:

Cockcroft, Swift, Turton, Smith, Kenny, Wands, S Powell trainer.

Front row left to right:

Froggatt, Robinson, Ward, Lowes, Tomlinson.

This was Jackie Robinsons last game for Sheffield Wednesday against Chesterfield on Saturday 21st September '46.

CONTENTS

PART TWO

by Eric Brodie

Chapter One

The Beginning

Hillsborough - Home to the Wednesday

This book has been written in two parts.

Part one tells you all about the personal life of Jackie Robinson, the man and the footballer.

It tells of his childhood, his love of his family and friends, his triumphs and heartaches, and all his ups and downs on and off the football pitch. These things can only be told by his family, that is why Alan, Jackie and Lillian's son in law, also a dedicated and loving fan since meeting and then marrying daughter Yvonne, wanted to put all he knew as a member of Jackie's family into this book.

Part two of this book has been written and compiled by myself, a lifelong fan of Jackie Robinson for over sixty three years. His name has always been magic to me, and still is. Over very many years, I have been in conversations with lots of football fans, some older and younger than myself who saw Jackie at his best or even past it, but their adoration and excitement for him has never ever gone. That is just how this man made you feel.

My biggest thrill in football was getting Jackie's autograph. After all these years, I can remember it as though it was yesterday. He was wearing a brown leather jacket, open necked shirt with his collar up, his wavy hair dropping on his forehead, a big smile on his face, and looking very handsome. Hero worship maybe, but I thought he was a really good-looking guy.

Lots of footballers around that period looked quite plain and very ordinary, not quite the Jackie Robinson look. In his Wednesday kit he looked the perfect footballer. To me and thousands more Wednesday'ites he was, and always has been. One of my greatest disappointments in football was that I never saw Jackie at his best. I had heard from my elder brother George, all about how brilliant he was and even in those early years when I had not seen him play, he was our idol and we worshiped him.

Being so young I didn't really understand about United and Wednesday'ites to that extent but after a year or so, hearing my brother always saying Robbo is fantastic, blue and white stripes look better than red and white, and Hillsborough is a better ground than Bramall Lane, I came to the conclusion that he must be a Wednesday'ite. So always believing everything that my brother told me was right, I knew I had to be like him and his influence stayed with me through my life until he sadly passed away in 1961 at the age of 33.

All my football memories came before that time because they were all shared George. We were deeply devoted and had great love and affection for each other. All our lives I remember him telling me all about the 1943 wartime cup final between Wednesday and Blackpool, saying that it wasn't really fair because Blackpool had a load of good players who were guesting for them. However, we drew 2-2 at their ground, and they only scored in the last minute. Jackie Robinson, who had just given Wednesday the lead, was badly injured.

A very bad injury to Ted Catlin, Wednesday's international full back meant they played for the last forty minutes with only ten men. Catlin was just a passenger on the wing.

The return leg at Hillsborough wasn't too good for Wednesday most of the team that had done so well at Blackpool had a poor day, though Jackie Robinson scored and with the score at 1-1 Dodds was fouled. He took the free kick himself scored and Wednesday had lost 2-1. The cup was lost and I and my brother's dreams were shattered. I wasn't at the match but my brother was. I think he cried for both of us and the Wednesday team but I believed he cried more for Jackie Robinson than anyone else.

That result really upset him.

The next final Jackie played in we saw it together. Wednesday beat Sheffield United in the 1944-45 county cup final. Although not as important as the Blackpool final it helped to heal the wounds for us.

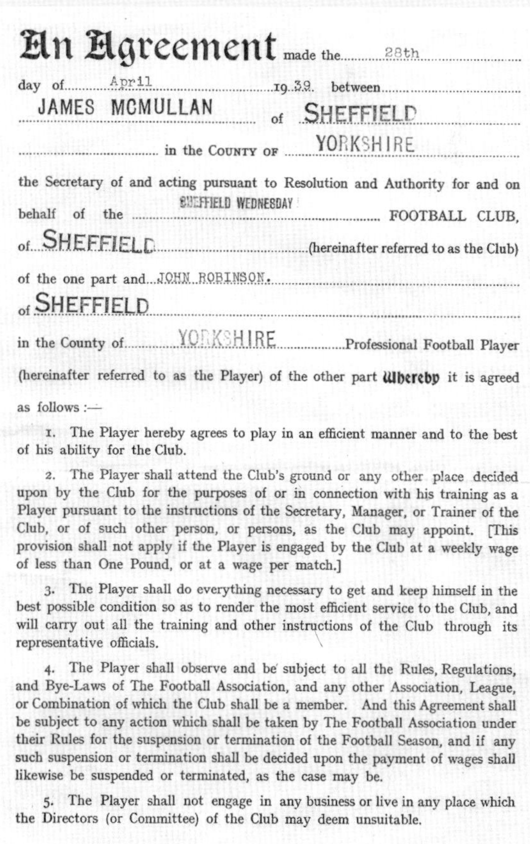

An Agreement made the 28th day of April 1939. between JAMES MCMULLAN of SHEFFIELD in the County of YORKSHIRE the Secretary of and acting pursuant to Resolution and Authority for and on behalf of the SHEFFIELD WEDNESDAY FOOTBALL CLUB, of SHEFFIELD (hereinafter referred to as the Club) of the one part and JOHN ROBINSON. of SHEFFIELD in the County of YORKSHIRE Professional Football Player (hereinafter referred to as the Player) of the other part Whereby it is agreed as follows :—

1. The Player hereby agrees to play in an efficient manner and to the best of his ability for the Club.

2. The Player shall attend the Club's ground or any other place decided upon by the Club for the purposes of or in connection with his training as a Player pursuant to the instructions of the Secretary, Manager, or Trainer of the Club, or of such other person, or persons, as the Club may appoint. [This provision shall not apply if the Player is engaged by the Club at a weekly wage of less than One Pound, or at a wage per match.]

3. The Player shall do everything necessary to get and keep himself in the best possible condition so as to render the most efficient service to the Club, and will carry out all the training and other instructions of the Club through its representative officials.

4. The Player shall observe and be subject to all the Rules, Regulations, and Bye-Laws of The Football Association, and any other Association, League, or Combination of which the Club shall be a member. And this Agreement shall be subject to any action which shall be taken by The Football Association under their Rules for the suspension or termination of the Football Season, and if any such suspension or termination shall be decided upon the payment of wages shall likewise be suspended or terminated, as the case may be.

5. The Player shall not engage in any business or live in any place which the Directors (or Committee) of the Club may deem unsuitable.

John Robinson's Agreement with Wednesday

Chapter Two

1943/44 - Season My first Visit to Hillsborough.

The 1943-44 season will always be a very special time for me.

It was the beginning of my real start as a Sheffield Wednesday supporter, watching them for probably the first time and actually seeing my idol Jackie Robinson playing on a regular basis.

He was all that I had thought and dreamt about for quite a few years.

I wasn't disappointed, Jackie was everything that I had expected. I don't think I could actually remember if he had played a blinder, but I think I can remember him scoring. I unfortunately missed quite a number of games this particular season as I spent a lot of the time in hospital. I suffered from T B (Tuberculosis) and I was in and out of hospitals and sanatoriums quite often.

I wasn't very strong as a youngster, and I suppose my mum wanted to protect me from the hustle and bustle of too many football crowds. In those wartime games we didn't always know what the teams would be, due to players being in the forces and being stationed all over different parts of the Country, not always being able to get leave. Some of them played for the teams where they were stationed, it seemed to work out fine for everyone.

In those days most players just wanted to play the game they loved, there were no agents who knew nothing about football and making loads of money advising them what and what not to do, as some do today. That's why in my opinion they will always be the real footballers who made the game of football what it was, the greatest game in the world.

Sadly I would prefer to watch the professional darts championship these days.

"Hat-trick" Expert Plays Against Scots

PERHAPS the chief feature of the Army team, announced yesterday, to meet Scotland at Hampden on February 20 is the return to big representative football of Robinson, Sheffield Wednesday international inside right, who has scored 24 goals, including six "hat-tricks" this season.

His display will not influence the England selectors for the Wales match at Wembley a week later because the England team will be chosen before the Hampden game is played.

But it will have a decided bearing on whether he plays against Scotland in April at Hampden.

Hagan, his great Sheffield United rival, who was the Army inside-right

England All Stars

Swift (Manchester City); Bacuzzi (Fulham), Compton (L.) (Arsenal); Britton (Everton), Cullis (Wolverhampton), Mercer (Everton); Birkett (Newcastle), Robinson (Wednesday), Westcott (Wolverhampton), Hagan (Sheffield United), Compton (D.) (Arsenal).

Reserves: Galley and Mullen (Wolverhampton).

at Leeds on Boxing Day, moves over to his natural position of inside-left.

Robinson was the star of the Berlin match of 1938. He was dropped after the Wales duel the following year and except for a couple of games with the Ack-Ack, has been passed over for representative matches.

Playing for the Army on January 26th 1943 Robinson scored four goals, in the 7-0 defeat of the Scots

In the 1944-5 season I remember Jackie Robinson missing quite a few matches, and although it spoilt my day a little, I still had other players that I liked.

I also loved the Hillsborough roar, which mostly came from the kop end where my brother and I stood. The roaring and chanting of the crowd was really thrilling and exciting for me, and it was said that all this was worth a goal to Wednesday if they needed one badly. Time and time again I found it was right. Times that we left the ground 10 minutes before the end of the match with Wednesday drawing or losing, we would hear this fantastic roar and we knew they had either won or at least saved the game.

Along with this famous roar there was also a team chorus that the fans always sang to urge the lads on, it went something like this,

Roll along Sheffield Wednesday roll along

Put the ball in the net where it belongs

When Robbo gets the ball

It's sure to be a goal

Roll along Sheffield Wednesday roll along.

Whenever Jackie got the ball he would start off on one of his dazzling runs and the crowd loved it, you could feel and sense the excitement. I have only ever known one other footballer in my life that ever gave me that kind of excitement and that was Derek Dooley, Wednesday's famous goal scoring centre forward of the early 1950's.

Though he was an entirely different player from Jackie, and I'm sure Derek would forgive me for saying he wasn't in the same class as Jackie as a footballer, but what an exciting player when he got the ball, you never knew what he would do with it.

Incidentally, Derek's idol was Jackie Robinson, which he is always proud to admit.

Derek Dooley

Chapter Three

Comparisons

Comparing different players was something that used to happen quite a lot, I suppose it still does. Most teams especially in the first division, had many great players, from the goalkeeper to the winger. Quite a number of them were internationals but there were a large number of them who weren't lucky enough to play for their country even though they were more than good enough. Because of that there were numerous arguments and comparisons from supporters of different clubs. In Sheffield the biggest argument was who was the best: Jackie Robinson or Jimmy Hagan.

Hagan was the Sheffield United international inside left who was quite a player, United fans loved him. He played in a few representative matches with Jackie and they played well together. There were some good press reports of their brilliant play.

All along at work or in the pubs fans of both sides would argue but I don't think anybody ever won as each set of fans believed their hero was the superior player.

I myself had seen plenty of both players, and probably more of Jimmy Hagan as I only lived two minutes walk from United's ground, plus the fact that Jimmy played lots of matches all through the 1950's, after Jackie had left for Sunderland. He then played for Lincoln City and retired after having the misfortune to break his leg after only nine matches.

I enjoyed watching Jimmy Hagan very much, he could beat two or three men and then deliver a perfect pass in an area of a few feet which made him a joy to watch but I always maintained that no one could compare the two players.

Jimmy Hagan

They were two very different types of footballers. Jackie was very fast with the ball, a brilliant body swerve and a great shot, he had to be moving, and in his prime he usually was like lightning. Jimmy was a slower player, always thinking more about what he wanted to do when he got the ball and where it was going to go. Jackie always knew what he was going to do with it as soon as he got it and he usually did.

In his early days, six hat tricks in the 1942-3 season explains it all.

Some people were inclined to think that Jackie was sometimes a little too selfish. That was when he wasn't quite as fast as he usually was, probably due to serving in the army during the war years. Also same as everyone else, the years were catching up on him, he had done it all for so long and so often that he always believed he still had it. If it came off he was brilliant but if he took on one defender to many that was when they called him selfish. Players with a style like Jackie had to be left to do their own stuff. I preferred his style to Jimmy Hagan's plus the fact that he was my number one footballer, but they were two marvellous footballers and it was nice we had them both in Sheffield for so many years. In my opinion I think United and Wednesday fans can consider themselves very fortunate but I suppose we will always keep on arguing and comparing, I don't mind that because it keeps their names and memories going on to the younger generations and that's good.

Though they have both sadly passed away, lets never forget them.

Jackie Robinson

Chapter Four

War over - back to business

The start of the 1945-6 season meant we were back to peacetime football. Players were slowly but surely getting demobbed and getting back to their lives in civvi street. They had been turned upside down as far as their football was concerned but like everyone else they had done what they had to do and gladly it was now over.

This war was no different from any other, lives were lost, among them many sporting celebrities and of course people from all walks of life. We owe all these people a great debt of gratitude.

On the football front, all the clubs were getting their players sorted out ready for this very special season.

I was looking forward to the season very much as there were lots of players I had read about but not yet had the chance to see.

I saw just about every game of the season so I saw all the great players and will always remember them with great admiration.

Wednesday's first home game was against Sunderland, I remember my father saying to me "keep your eye on Raich Carter, he's a great player."

This I did and I wasn't disappointed, he played a great game even though his team lost 6-3. The joy of the afternoon was the fact that my idol Jackie Robinson had a great game and along with Alf Rodgers scored a great hat-trick. I was very fortunate to have had the opportunity to see Raich Carter play quite a few times, firstly with Sunderland , then with Derby County and in the end with Hull City. I would always put him as one of my top greatest players.

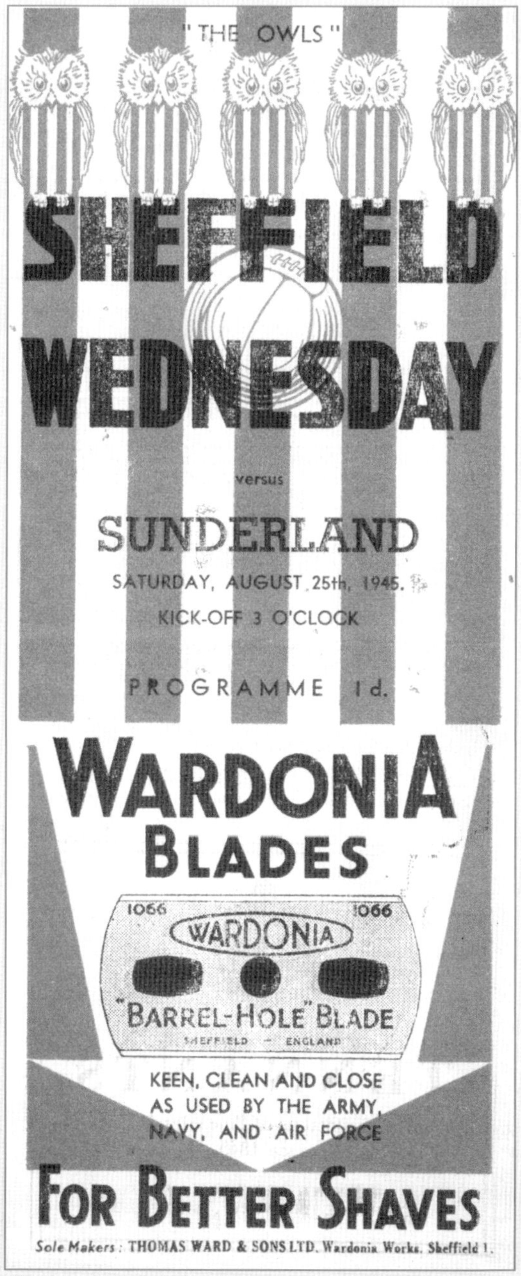

Ironically, the first game after the war was Wednesday versus Sunderland

There was also a little extra joy for me this particular season. I loved the match programmes, they were then and even now as a programme collector still my favourites.

Sheffield United's were almost identical but the two things that made Wednesday's better was the colour of blue and white but most of all, was the magic name of Jackie Robinson appearing in most of them.

I was so obsessed with Jackie and how he looked, that I used to wet my hair with soapy water, press it into a big wave, and when the soap had dried I would then comb it out and I had the famous Jackie Robinson wave hanging over my forehead. With my open collar pulled up, it all seemed serious stuff for me in those early days of my life, but I can have a laugh about it now.

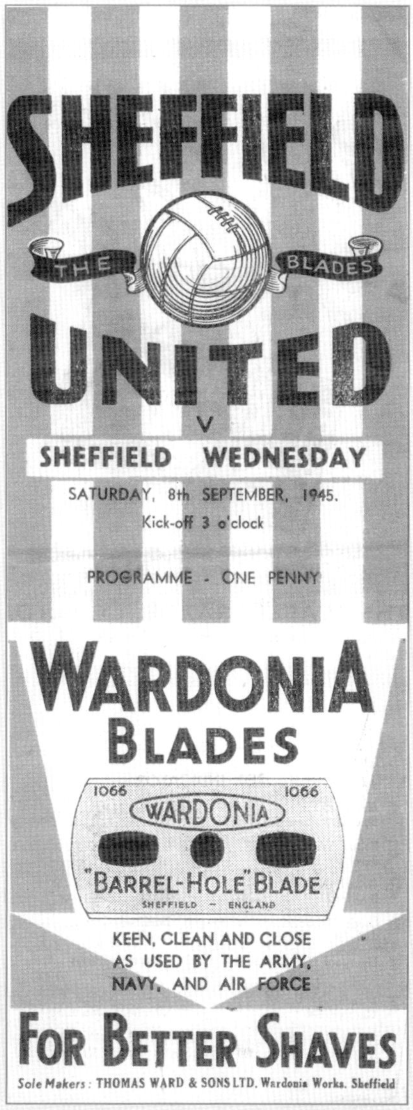

Sheffield United programme almost identical in layout

Various Wednesday programmes

Chapter Five

The County Cup

Every year both Sheffield clubs, along with Rotherham United, Barnsley and Doncaster Rovers, played a knock-out tournament for a trophy named the Sheffield and Hallamshire County Cup.

Starting around the early 1920's, it carried on until around the late 1970's or early 1980's.

During the draw for the knockout matches I seem to remember that one of the five clubs was awarded a bye, because of the odd number of teams. Each rival teams supporters welcomed the competition, especially if their season had not been very exhilarating, due to no promotion prospects, a long fight against relegation, or even no exciting F A cup run. Every match would also be a local derby, so the climax of the season would be "Let's win the County Cup". The 1944-5 season was fondly remembered because it was my first ever presence at a cup final of any kind. I was lucky enough to be at each leg of the final, Wednesday v United. The first leg was at Bramall Lane where I saw Wednesday win 3-1, Jackie Robinson scored the first goal and played well. The second leg was even better for us, Wednesday won 4-2 at Hillsborough and Jackie again scored the first goal.

County cup final programme 1945

That is a day I will always remember, along with hundreds of Wednesday fans including my brother we ran on to the pitch after the game to acclaim their victory.

The Wednesday team presented themselves to their fans and Jackie Robinson who was captain held the cup aloft. Nobody outside South Yorkshire really understood what winning the County Cup meant to us. For myself, it was my first Cup Final, we had beaten United and my idol Jackie Robinson was showing it of to us all. What more could I ask for. I did feel a little sorry for the United fans, as their team had lost in a two-leg semi-final in the last wartime F.A.Cup competition to an Aston Villa team that included Wednesday's former captain Ronnie Starling of the 1935 F.A. Cup Final winning team.

Robinson (Wednesday captain) receiving the Sheffield County Cup after defeating Sheffield United 4-2 in the second leg at Hillsborough. Wednesday also won the first leg at Bramall Lane 3-1. Jackie, inevitably, scored a goal in both games.

Chapter Six

Shattered Dreams

The 1946-7 season seemed to come around very quickly, as I hoped it would do.

I had lots of expectations and dreams of Sheffield Wednesday doing great things, and looking forward very much to see my great idol Jackie Robinson helping them to achieve it all.

Jackie was in dispute with the Owls!

Sadly, everything started going wrong after a few games, Wednesday had lost four out of seven played - drew one and won only two, conceding 18 goals and scoring only 12 in reply.

Jackie had scored 6 of this total, scoring in 5 of the 7 matches played.

Worse was to follow.

During this early period of the season, came the shattering reports that Jackie had got some kind of dispute with the club, and a transfer looked likely. I kept my fingers crossed for quite a while, believing and desperately hoping that Wednesday could not possibly let our Jackie leave Hillsborough, the place where he was worshiped by thousands of supporters. He couldn't leave, he had been for many years, and still was, the biggest name, the most exciting player and everyone's favourite. At that time Jackie had lost some of that brilliance he once had, but he could always give us little reminders that he still had it, showing his skill and goal scoring ability, that thrilled us all so much for so many years. We didn't want to lose him. The first few results had not been very good for Wednesday but when we came to watch the team against Chesterfield at Hillsborough on the 21st of September, we didn't dream that it would be the last game that Jackie would be playing for Wednesday. Sadly it was. Sheffield Wednesday lost 1-0 and Jackie had a poor game, maybe the thoughts of leaving his teammates, his friends, Hillsborough, and especially his adoring fans was on his mind. In fact, all the team played badly that afternoon and I will always believe in my own mind that it rubbed off on them all. Even though the score was only 1-0, Chesterfield should have won more easily.

October the 11th 1946, the newspaper headline we had all been dreading came.

Jackie Robinson signs for Sunderland.

All his fans were shattered, I, along with my brother George, were devastated. How could he go? What would Wednesday do without him? What would we do without our beloved Jackie? We all had been hoping and praying that he would stay. I hated Sunderland football club for taking Jackie from us. I believed that things would never be the same again at Hillsborough. Even the slight thought crossed my mind that I would stop watching Wednesday. I was feeling really upset and felt like retaliating in some way just to hurt myself and to show everyone how upset I was.

I had always watched United play, even before I had started watching Wednesday but once a regular visitor at Hillsborough, I went alternately to both grounds. This way I had the great privilege of having the opportunity of seeing all the great footballers that in my opinion were the greatest, always will be, and who put so much more back into the game than they ever took out of it. I did manage to stay away from both grounds for a few matches, usually playing football myself. Even though I impersonated my idol Jackie, with my collar up, and sporting my famous Jackie Robinson wave, I thought I looked great but played badly.

I'm sorry to admit, I was never that much of a footballer but I did have my moments and I really loved playing as well as watching this great game. A few weeks went by and reluctantly I had been quietly checking, first how Jackie was doing with his new team Sunderland, then seeing whether Wednesday had lost again.

The sad news was that Jackie was doing all right with his new team, and Wednesday were still playing badly. After drawing their first game 2-2 away at Millwall without him, they lost the next four matches. I believe I was probably thinking, it serves them right for selling Jackie and shattering my dreams.

Wednesday finished in 20th position in the 2nd division table with the embarrassing statistics

Home						Away					
P	W	D	L	F	A	W	D	L	F	A	Pts
42	10	5	6	39	28	2	3	16	28	60	32

Not a very impressive record after finishing 5th the previous season and I'm in no doubt that anyone who reads this book will know who I thought was to blame for it all.

As I got older I suppose I learned that lots of things happen within the business of any football club, sometimes not always pleasing to the fans and we have to accept that in the end clubs and players have to do what is right for them.

Chapter Seven

Wednesday without Jackie

J. ROBINSON (SHEFFIELD WEDNESDAY)

During the disappointing 1946-7 season Wednesday tried very hard to find a replacement for Jackie but that was quite a tall order, not just because of his ability but also his popularity.

The first player who was thrust into the number 8 shirt was Arnold Lowes.

He had been playing the first few games at inside left with Jackie at inside right and although he was a decent player and had played in a few other positions at the club he could never fill Jackie's role on the forward line.

To be honest it wasn't going to be easy for anyone to do.

During this time, the team was still struggling, losing four matches out of 6, drawing 1 and winning just 1 game.

The season carried on in a similar sort of pattern until about the beginning of November when Wednesday signed George Hunt from Spurs, again trying to fill the gap left by Jackie.

Hunt was quite an experienced player and had been around for a few years so Wednesday were hoping they had solved their problem . With the arrival of a young centre forward namely Jimmy Dailey from Third Lanark they were hoping to bring some improvement to the team, get some better results, and also to try and satisfy the supporters, probably hoping the loss of their idol would soon be forgotten. Some hope!

These signings did make a slight improvement but there were still lots of problems for the club.

George Hunt

Saturday 1st March Wednesday played Spurs at Hillsborough and included a new signing from West Bromwich Albion, a Welsh international wing half named Dougie Witcomb, who cost them £6000, and as we all found out in the following weeks it was a great buy and it probably saved Wednesday from dropping down into the third division. They won the Spurs game 5-1 with Jimmie Dailey getting a hat-trick and went on to their best run of the season playing 14 games, winning 6, losing 6 and drawing 2.

Dougie Witcomb

Staying in division 2 had given us all some excitement during the last final weeks, plus a few new faces but I really think most of us were glad that the season was over.

We had all missed our idol Jackie Robinson; Wednesday didn't look the same and Hillsborough didn't look the same either when he wasn't around.

It didn't always bother me so much if he had a poor game, just the presence of this man on the pitch was enough to make me happy, but alas, he was no longer there.

Chapter Eight
The Turn Around

The 1947-48 season duly arrived, maybe with a lot of luck we might have a good season and be good enough to get ourselves promotion. It was in October of this season that Eric Taylor the Wednesday Secretary Manager made one of his best ever signings.
That signing gave us all hope for the future.
We had to accept that Jackie had gone, we were also Wednesday'ites so we had to support the team and the manager. The player that came to us was Eddie Quigley from Bury, who turned out to be one of Wednesday's best ever bargains at £12,000. Eddie had just about everything, a good strong player, who could work his way through a defence, and lay on splendid passes to his teammates. He was also a good positional player with a great shot, and a prolific goalscorer, as his record as a Wednesday player speaks for itself, 78 games, and 52 goals, very impressive!
He became a very strong favourite with most of the Wednesday fans, myself included but he never attained the heights of adoration and hero worship as our Jackie did.
To his credit, he wore Jackie's number 8 shirt with great pride and commitment and I feel sure that Jackie would have appreciated it. Along with the joy of Eddie Quigley arriving we had the sadness of Jimmy Dailey leaving, and joining Birmingham City. I had taken quite a liking to Jimmy, I liked to see him chase the long balls and he was very fast and created lots of excitement, especially when he got to the ball before the goalkeeper.

Jimmy Dailey

Eddie Quigley

Jimmy Dailey's record of 41 appearances scoring 25 goals is no bad feat, especially when you realise that 13 goals from 17 games in the 1946-7 helped to keep Wednesday in the 2nd division.

This was quite a busy time for Sheffield Wednesday and their manager Eric Taylor. With Dailey not being in the team regularly, Wednesday bought Clarrie Jordan the record goal scoring centre forward from Doncaster Rovers. At the end of the season we had finished a respectable 4th position in division 2, just missing promotion which I am glad to say they did achieve 2 years later, finishing 2nd.

Eric Taylor, Manager and Secretary

Sadly the following year they were relegated, and throughout the 1950's they were up and down like a yo-yo, thus earning the knick-name the yo-yo team.

All through these years my brother George and myself gave the Sheffield Wednesday team all our undying loyalty and support.

We had exciting seasons, one year fighting relegation, and the next year gaining promotion. 1952-3 was the most exciting in this period, that was the great Derek Dooley era. Something we will never ever forget but that's another story or a fantastic fairy tale. Derek Dooley was the first player to give me that same kind of excitement that was lost at Hillsborough after Jack Robinson had left. Two fantastic legends and so different but I am so pleased that I had the chance to see plenty of them both, I wont ever stop talking about them or ever forget them.

My brother George and myself, Eric Brodie

Chapter Nine

Jackie leaves Sunderland

All the time that Jackie had been at Sunderland I was enjoying all the ups and downs of the Wednesday team, but keeping a very watchful eye on how Jackie was playing, and if he had scored.

I don't think I can ever recall Jackie playing against Wednesday after he had left them. He did, however, play quite a few games for them 85 in all, and scored 34 goals, another impressive record, all in the top flight of the 1st division.

By the 1948-49 season first team matches were getting fewer due to the fact that at this time in his career he was about 32 or so years of age and even though some of the old magic was there and the Sunderland fans had enjoyed it all, it was getting harder for him to keep it up week in and week out in the 1st division.

Jackie's inside forward partner was Len Shackleton who was younger and also getting recognition as an England international player. They had been a very formidable force for Sunderland but the club then signed another young brilliant inside forward named Ivor Broadis so by this time things were looking rather bleak for Jackie.

An opportunity came for him to join Lincoln City as player coach, which seemed a good move for him and would have kept him in football doing what he loved for a few more years so he accepted the post. It was also a good move for my brother and myself as it was nearer to Sheffield and we were able to see our old hero playing again.

We only managed to see a couple of games at Lincoln but even though he had changed I could see everything there that I had always loved about him. Just watching him on the pitch, walking, running, dribbling, passing and shooting brought all those lovely magic memories back.

After nine games Jackie sadly broke his leg, and left Lincoln. For quite a few years after that I didn't know what had happened to him but a few things were happening in my own life in those early years of the 1950's.

Jackie Robinson Stretcher Case

Jackie Robinson scored a double for Lincoln against Wrexham, but whilst scoring his second goal he received an injury and was carried off on a stretcher.

He was taken to Lincoln Hospital for an X-ray examination of his leg.

Chapter Ten

Life Without Jackie

After Jackie had left Lincoln City football club, I wrote to both them and Sunderland asking them if they could put me in touch with him but I never had a reply from either of them, which saddened me very much.

I so much wanted to write to him and thank him for all the excitement and pleasure that he had given to me, my brother George, and also all the many millions of football fans all over the country and probably in different parts of the world. I would also have liked to have told him how much influence he had poured into my life but sadly it wasn't to be because I just couldn't locate him.

The early fifties were quite memorable for me especially the 15th March 1952 because I was married on that day, it was and has been, the happiest day of my life.

I had met Barbara in August 1947. She was 15 years old and still at grammar school, I was 16 and working.

I met her when I went to play football near to where she lived. She was watching the game and instantly fell madly in love with this tall, handsome, curly haired goalscoring centre forward. Sadly she finished up with a date with a not so tall, straight haired, not such a goal scoring centre forward but sporting a lovely Jackie Robinson quiff, yes that was ME!

Babs as I always called her was the most beautiful, most loved, and loveliest person that I have ever met in my life and I was lucky to have been married to her for 41 years before she sadly passed away in 1993. Everyone who ever met her just fell in love with her. I have dedicated this paragraph to Babs because she probably heard me talk about and listened to the name of Jackie Robinson more than anyone else I could ever imagine apart from Jackie's family.

Sheffield Star On Transfer

WEST BROM. MAY SECURE JACKIE ROBINSON

By ALBERT BOOTH

ON and on, up and up goes the Soccer transfer craze. Next five figure fee to change hands will be for Jackie Robinson, Sheffield Wednesday and England inside-right. He has been placed on the open list for competition.

Once more a domestic issue arises. The housing problem has presented difficulties which the Wednesday club have been unable to overcome in wishing to have the player live near headquarters.

Hence the decision to part with Robinson, who is residing at Newcastle and has been doing his training with the United club at St. James's Park.

A fortnight ago West Bromwich Albion approached Wednesday about signing Robinson.

The answer they got was "Nothing doing!"

The request was renewed last week-end. Again "No!"

But yesterday Wednesday decided to put Robinson on transfer.

They communicated with the Albion and told them that their bid would receive first consideration, and last night awaited a reply, following a board meeting at West Bromwich.

Robinson joined Wednesday in 1934-1935 season and made his first ppearance in the first team as a puth in a League match against est Bromwich Albion shortly fore the clubs met in the Cup al that year.

e played for England against s, and also in four matches on ontinent.

JACKIE ROBINSON

A speculative story about Jackie being transferred to West Bromwich Albion

Babs with Eric, she listened to plenty of stories about Jackie Robinson.

Chapter Eleven

Jackie's Teammates

On nearing the final part of 'The Jackie Robinson Story' I cannot end without a dedication to the many Sheffield Wednesday players who were teammates and friends of Jackie. Many of these footballers were also a big part of my early years as a spectator and a dedicated Owls supporter. Their names still bring fond memories to me and remind me also of the happy and exciting times I spent with my brother George watching them play.

Rimmer, Thompson, Mathews Robinson and Hooper

Through the early years of Jackie's career, the wartime era and then his final years at Hillsborough Jackie and his teammates brought us many happy and memorable Saturday afternoons, something we can always remember. In those days words like loyalty, effort and dedication, to the club and fans, were something that professional footballers believed in and for the few years they played they gave it all, and enjoyed every moment of it.

Joe Cockcroft leads the Wednesday team out against Cardiff at Ninian Park.

Nobody made much money in those days but if they looked after their coppers and had been careful in their lifestyle a lot of the players bought pubs and others bought little shops. It is also sad to think of the many players who delighted the crowds week in and week out went back to work in the pits or took on badly paid labouring work. This was because some of them had missed out on apprenticeships due to football commitments. In those days there were no such things as footballer's agents as there are today. There was no need for them. In those days football was a sport not a business as in my opinion it is to day. I am glad to say I believe that most if not all of the old standards made football the greatest game and sport in the world.

In this chapter of Jackie's team mates, there is one player who I have to say was top of the list in my opinion, of dedication, loyalty, always gave everything he could possibly give to the club and the fans. His dream was to follow his fathers footsteps and play for Sheffield Wednesday, this dream he achieved and he turned out to be one of the Owl's greatest players and his loyalty was unsurpassed; a few England honours also came his way, which were richly deserved, he was a credit to his family, Wednesday, his fans, and more than anything to himself. I would think that any old Wednesday supporter or anyone having read any of the clubs books or their history would know without a doubt the player in question is Redfern Froggatt.

Red Froggatt

Topical Times cards depicting Sheffield Wednesday regulars, Starling, Catlin, Russell and Hooper

J Thompson

L Massarella

They played alongside Jackie

G Napier

A Lowes

E Packard

W Pickering

E Rimmer

H Swift

F Herbert

T Ward

W Millership

J Nibloe

F Westlake

D Hunt

D Goodfellow

A Morton

J Brown

R Smith

One thing I must say about one aspect of his play, if there was any other player who could execute the long ball through the inside of the full back to the feet of the winger running into the penalty, I honestly never saw him, maybe the nearest to him was probably Johnny Haynes of Fulham and England. I could very easily go on writing all the good things about Redfern Froggatt and jogging my memory box, I have many special memories of this great footballer.

Jackie in training with some of his team mates

On the few occasions my wife Barbara went to watch Wednesday with me she only wanted to see one man, that was Redfern. Then she would complain saying that she wished he would smile more instead of looking so sad.

Moving on, my list of Jackie's team mates include the goalkeepers Jack Brown, Derek Goodfellow, Roy Smith and Albert Morton. Though Morton was not a world beater he was a fine goalkeeper and very spectacular. The limited times I saw him play I just loved watching him.

A couple of the many cards of Jackie Robinson issued by newspapers or the cigarette/tobacco companies of the 30s and 40s.

Without these items given away free by the aforementioned companies we would have very few pictures of footballers in this era.

Full backs: there were Albert"Jumbo"Ashley, Billy Pickering, Frank Westlake, Ted Catlin, and my favourite, Hugh Swift. Barring injury which finally ended his playing career many believed he would have played for England. Sheffield Wednesday, as with inside forwards always seem to have been blessed with very good half backs and in some of Jackie's teams there were players like Horace Burrows a player from the victorious 1935 cup winning team, Dave Russell and Joe Cockroft. Joe Cockroft a great player from West Ham United who was a guest player for the Owls during the war years was once quoted as saying that although Jackie Robinson was a great player there were odd occasions when Joe had words with Jackie about being too selfish and saying that there were other players in the team. Joe Cockroft later went to Sheffield United, then retired but stayed in Sheffield.

Wednesday in Hoops - pictured just after the war in their unusual strip - Jackie Robinson on the left.

Wednesday team after Jackie's departure to Sunderland

Len Massarella was a stocky hard working winger with a powerful shot when on his best form was very direct and dangerous and scored plenty of goals. Les Tomlinson nick named "shadows" was another of my favourite players. On his day he was a world-beater, his casual slouchy style made him look a little sluggish at times but the crowd loved him.

Tommy Ward was the type of player every manager would love to have on his books. Apart from being blessed with unfounded energy and enthusiasm, he just loved playing football and played in every position for his club including goal.

Other wingers who played in the teams with Jackie were Mark Hooper who was a great player in quite a few positions and unlucky not to have been capped and his opposite wing man Ellis Rimmer, another good player who was capped four times for England. Rimmer and Hooper scored many goals between them and both played a memorable part in some of Wednesday's great triumphs. Ellis Rimmer had the distinction of scoring in every round of the F A Cup and scored twice in the final at Wembley. There was also W. Fallon, G. B. Drury and Bill Reynolds a Rochdale player who guested for Wednesday during the war and played in the 1943 wartime Cup Final.

The inside forward as with the half back line was swelled with talented players. Apart from Jackie himself there were Ronnie Starling, a great footballer, captain and an England international. Charlie Napier, a Scottish international who was a very tricky player with good passing qualities and possessed great shooting ability. He and Jackie formed a very dangerous and exciting partnership. Jackie Thompson who was with Wednesday for many years from 1933-1946 was a tremendous inside forward but due to the wealth of talent in that position he didn't get the chances he deserved. Alf Rodgers another of Jackie's inside partners was another player who found it hard to get first team football, when he did he always took his chances and played well partnering Jackie around 22 times. Alan Driver also deserves a mention, he played in quite a few positions for Wednesday and although not one of the top players he played his part well and like Tommy Ward was a good man to have at the club. Arnold Lowes another great clubman for Wednesday played in many positions for the club. It was with Lowes and his wife that a young Jackie Robinson boarded when he first came to Sheffield. I had the pleasure of having a couple of nice meetings with Mrs Lowes talking about her husband, some of the players I have mentioned and most of all she told me about a young Jackie and Lillian Robinson before and after they were married. She said Jackie was a happy good-natured young man and that Lillian was very beautiful with long hair.

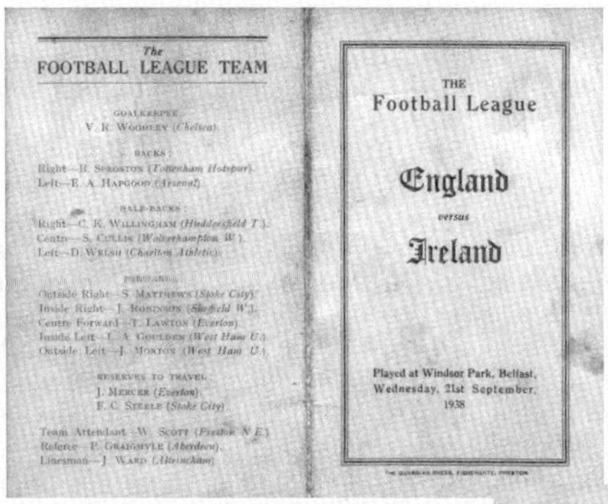
The FOOTBALL LEAGUE TEAM

GOALKEEPER: V. R. Woodley (Chelsea).

BACKS: Right—B. Sproston (Tottenham Hotspur). Left—E. A. Hapgood (Arsenal).

HALF-BACKS: Right—C. K. Willingham (Huddersfield T.). Centre—S. Cullis (Wolverhampton W.). Left—D. Welsh (Charlton Athletic).

FORWARDS: Outside Right—S. Matthews (Stoke City). Inside Right—J. Robinson (Sheffield W.). Centre Forward—T. Lawton (Everton). Inside Left—L. A. Goulden (West Ham U.). Outside Left—J. Morton (West Ham U.).

RESERVES TO TRAVEL: J. Mercer (Everton). F. C. Steele (Stoke City).

Team Attendant—W. Scott (Preston N.E.). Referee—P. Craigmyle (Aberdeen). Linesman—J. Ward (Altrincham).

THE Football League

England versus Ireland

Played at Windsor Park, Belfast, Wednesday, 21st September, 1938

Jackie Robinson's timetable for the game against Ireland at Windsor Park, Belfast.

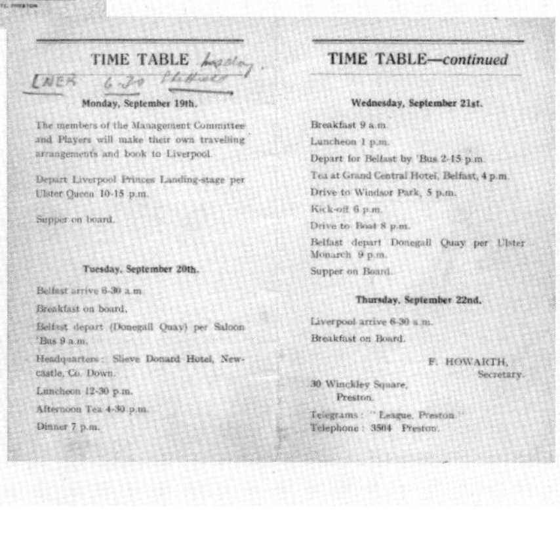
TIME TABLE

Monday, September 19th.

The members of the Management Committee and Players will make their own travelling arrangements and book to Liverpool.

Depart Liverpool Princes Landing-stage per Ulster Queen 10-15 p.m.

Supper on board.

Tuesday, September 20th.

Belfast arrive 6-30 a.m.

Breakfast on board.

Belfast depart (Donegall Quay) per Saloon 'Bus 9 a.m.

Headquarters: Slieve Donard Hotel, Newcastle, Co. Down.

Luncheon 12-30 p.m.

Afternoon Tea 4-30 p.m.

Dinner 7 p.m.

TIME TABLE—continued

Wednesday, September 21st.

Breakfast 9 a.m.

Luncheon 1 p.m.

Depart for Belfast by 'Bus 2-15 p.m.

Tea at Grand Central Hotel, Belfast, 4 p.m.

Drive to Windsor Park, 5 p.m.

Kick-off 6 p.m.

Drive to Boat 8 p.m.

Belfast depart Donegall Quay per Ulster Monarch 9 p.m.

Supper on Board.

Thursday, September 22nd.

Liverpool arrive 6-30 a.m.

Breakfast on Board.

F. HOWARTH, Secretary.

30 Winckley Square, Preston.

Telegrams: "League, Preston." Telephone: 3504 Preston.

The centre forward position was at certain times a problem for the club. Quite a few of the Wednesday players around the 1937-1946 era had a go at playing in that position. Neil Dewar a Scottish international played along side Jackie a few times but moved on in 1937. Other players were Douglas Hunt, Frank Melling, Jack Lindsey and one or two who played just a few games such as W. Aveyard and W. Ibbottson.

Sheffield Wednesday FA Cup winning side showing off the trophy at Hillsborough

Douglas Hunt who played between Jackie and Charlie Napier was a very fine player scoring plenty of goals. He holds the record of scoring six goals in one match, which is still a Wednesday record. In his first two seasons between 1937 and 1939 he scored 31 goals in 47 appearances. Frank Melling an amateur who played during the war years scored 35 goals in 55 matches and was also a very good cricketer. A few more players who played along side Jackie were J. Nibloe, H. Goodson, H. Hanford, A. Wands, C. Turton, F. Herbert, E. Packard, T. Gale, W. Millership, O. Fox, N. Roebuck, I. Lewis, R. Rhodes and a few who played the odd game or two and I apologise if I haven't mentioned their names.

In the last seven matches of the 1943/44 season a young goalkeeper Harry Donaldson of Notts County guested for Wednesday. The following season Wednesday played at Notts County but only turned up with 9 men so they signed on Donaldson just before kick-off and played him at outside right therefore playing with 10 men. Jackie arrived at half time and never took part in the game. The Owls lost the match 2-0. In the return match at Hillsborough the following week Wednesday won 6-1. Donaldson only played 2 more matches for the Owls.

Sheffield Wednesday FA Cup winners.

left: Ronnie Starling shaking hands with the WBA captain

right: 90 minutes later carrying the FA cup around Wembley. Ronnie Starling was the last Wednesday captain to lift this illustrious trophy.

Chapter Twelve

The Legacy

I have now arrived at my final chapter.

I have written about the joys and excitement that Jackie Robinson brought to us all. There were happy times and sad times but none as sad as when I read that Jackie had passed away. For a few days after I heard this news I couldn't stop thinking about him and all my memories of Jackie and all I have written about in this book came flooding back. I never stop talking about Jackie when discussing football and even to this day lots of people talk about him with enjoyment and excitement even though some of them never saw him play but just heard their Fathers or Grandfathers talk about him. Even now the name Jackie Robinson or "Robbo" as he was nicknamed still sounds magic to the old and young Wednesday supporters. I sincerely hope that you enjoyed reading my Jackie Robinson story.

Jackie "the nice guy" in army attire attending his corporals, Joe Warringtons wedding as best man. Warrington was a Blackpool player who was a teammate of Jackie in the army side

Jackie Robinson

ituaries from the
effield Star:

ght:
ticle by Keith Farnsworth
ted August 2nd 1972

r right:
ticle by Peter Markie
ted August 1st 1972

Memories of Jackie

By KEITH FARNSWORTH

Jackie Robinson, who has died at his Shiremoor Northumberland, home, won a special place in the hearts of Sheffield Wednesday supporters in the years immediately before and during the Second World War.

An inside-forward, he had the knack of being in the right place at the right time to score a vital goal: and in his best season (1942-3) he bagged 35, including six hat-tricks, to help Wednesday reach the League North Cup final.

But he had something more than a goal-sense: his skill and craft were such that many of those who saw him still cherish the memory and claim he would have earned more than four England caps if there had not been such a surfeit of brilliant inside-forwards available.

The story goes that Wednesday manager Billy Walker went to a Tyneside junior match to watch another youngster, but couldn't take his eyes off Robinson. The teenager was signed and made his League debut at West Brom — in borrowed boots boots belonging to another legendary figure, Ronnie Starling, who stood down because of a late injury.

Goal-knack

That was in April, 1935. Within 18 months Robinson was a first team regular, and in his first full season played in an international trial.

In May, 1937, he won his first England cap, scoring on his debut against Finland in Helsinki. He partnered Stanley Matthews in England's matches against Germany, Switzerland and Wales in 1938.

Robinson, with the subtle swerve, the unexpected burst of speed, and the goal-knack, scored 38 Football League and FA Cup goals in addition to the 93 in the war years. These figures tell only part of the story of a "character" who was the boyhood idol of present team manager Derek Dooley and thousands who still talk about him wherever old Wednesdayites gather.

He moved to Sunderland in October, 1946, and his colleagues at Roker Park included present Chesterfield manager, Jim McGuigan.

Former Owls star Jackie Robinson dies, aged 55

By Peter Markie

JACKIE Robinson, one of the all-time Sheffield Wednesday greats, died yesterday at his home village of Shiremoor, Northumberland, aged 55.

Wednesday's assistant secretary Eric England said this afternoon: "Jackie had been ill for the last two years.

"He was in my view the finest inside forward ever to play for Wednesday. A goalscorer, master of control and a phenomenal body swerve made him a great among greats."

Jackie's arrival at Hillsborough is a famous milestone in their history.

Spotted in the North East, he was brought down by my manager Billy Walker and played before he was 17.

This was the Easter Monday game with West Bromwich Albion — five days before the Owls-Albion Wembley Cup Final in 1934.

Robinson was an instant hit and stayed that way with the Hillsborough fans. Within a few months he was called up by England and played against Finland when he was only 17 years and nine months.

He played in England's famous victory over Germany in Berlin in 1938 — and refused to give the Nazi salute before the kick-off.

The war, in fact, checked a brilliant career for he was at his prime in 1939.

During the '39-46 spell, he scored 93 goals for the Owls. In 1942-43, he did the hat-trick six times in a tally of 35.

Wanted by a string of clubs during his career at Hillsborough, he joined Sunderland in 1946.

PLAYING CAREER RECORD WITH
SHEFFIELD WEDNESDAY

1934-35 (DIV.1)

40 APR.22	(A)	WEST BROM.A	D	1-1	1G	10

1935-36 (DIV.1)

9 OCT.5	(A)	BRENTFORD	D	2-2		8
17 NOV.30	(H)	CHELSEA	W	4-1		8
18 DEC.7	(A)	BLACKBURN.R	L	2-3		8
19 DEC.14	(H)	STOKE.C	L	0-1		8
41 APR.25	(H)	LIVERPOOL	D	0-0		8

1936-37 (DIV.1.)

9 OCT.3	(H)	PRESTON.N.E	L	0-1		10
14 NOV.7	(H)	GRIMSBY. T	W	2-1	1G	8
15 NOV.14	(A)	LIVERPOOL	D	2-2		8
16 NOV.21	(H)	LEEDS UTD.	L	1-2		8
17 NOV.28	(A)	BIRMINGHAM	D	1-1		8
18 DEC.5	(H)	MIDDLESBOROUGH W		1-0		8
19 DEC.19	(H)	MANCHESTER C	W	5-1	2G	8
20 DEC.25	(A)	BRENTFORD	L	1-2	1G	8
21 DEC.26	(A)	SUNDERLAND	L	1-2		8
22 DEC.28	(H)	BRENTFORD	L	0-2		8
23 JAN.2	(H)	WOLVES	L	1-3		8
24 JAN.9	(A)	DERBY C	L	2-3		8
3 JAN.16	(H)	PORT VALE	W	2-0	1G	8
26 FEB.3	(A)	PORTSMOUTH	L	0-1		8
27 FEB.6	(A)	PRESTON NE	D	1-1		8
28 FEB.13	(H)	ARSENAL	D	0-0		8
29 FEB.20	(H)	CHELSEA	D	1-1		8
30 MAR.6	(H)	CHARLTON A	W	3-1	1G	8
31 MAR.13	(A)	GRIMSBY T	L	1-5		8
32 MAR.20	(H)	LIVERPOOL	L	1-2		8
33 MAR.26	(A)	BOLTON W	L	0-1		8
34 MAR.27	(A)	LEEDS U	D	1-1		10
35 MAR.29	(H)	BOLTON W	W	2-0		10
36 APR.3	(H)	BIRMINGHAM	L	0-3		10
37 APR.5	(A)	STOKE C	L	0-1		8
38 APR.10	(A)	MIDDLESBOROUGH	L	0-2		7
39 APR.10	(H)	WEST BROM A	L	2-3		9
40 APR.21	(A)	WEST BROM A	W	3-2		8
41 APR.24	(A)	MANCHESTER C	L	1-4		8
42 MAY.1	(A)	HUDDERSFIELD	L	0-1		8

1937-38 (DIV.2.)

1 AUG.28	(A)	CHESTERFIELD	L	0-1		10
2 SEP.2	(H)	FULHAM	W	2-1	1G	8
3 SEP.4	(H)	SWANSEA T	D	1-1		8
4 SEP.6	(A)	FULHAM	D	0-0		8
5 SEP. 11	(A)	NORWICH C	L	1-3		8
8 SEP.25	(A)	BRADFORD	D	1-1		8
9 OCT.2	(H)	WEST HAM U	W	1-0		8
10OCT.9	(A)	SOUTHAMPTON	L	2-5		8
11 OCT. 16	(H)	SHEFFIELD U	L	0-1		8
12OCT.23	(A)	MAN U	L	0-1		7
13OCT.30	(H)	STOCKPORT C	D	3-3	1G	8
14 NOV.6	(A)	BARNSLEY	L	1-4		8
15 NOV. 13	(H)	LUTON T	W	4-0	1G	10
18DEC.4	(A)	NEWCASTLE U	L	0-1		8
19 DEC. 11	(H)	BURY	W	2-0		8
20 DEC. 18	(A)	BURNLEY	D	1-1	1G	8
30 FEB.26	(A)	SHEFFIELD U	L	1-2		8
31MAR.5	(H)	MANCHESTER U	L	1-3		8
32 MAR.12	(A)	STOCKPORT C	L	1-2		8
33 MAR.19	(H)	BARNSLEY	L	0-1		8
34 MAR.26	(A)	LUTON T	D	2-2	1G	8
35 APR.2	(H)	COVENTRY	W	2-1	1G	8
36 APR.9	(A)	NOTTINGHAM F	W	1-0		8
37 APR. 16	(H)	NEWCASTLE U	W	3-0	1G	8
38 APR. 18	(A)	BLACKBURN R	L	0-1		8
39 APR. 19	(H)	BLACKBURN R	W	2-1		8
40 APR.23	(A)	BURY	L	0-2		8
41 APR.30	(H)	BURNLEY	W	2-1		8
42 MAY.7	(A)	TOTTENHAM H	W	2-1		8

1938-39 (DIV.2.)

1 AUG.27	(H)	BURY	W	2-0	1G	8
2 AUG.29	(A)	TOTTENHAM H	D	3-3	1G	8
3 SEP.3	(A)	WEST HAM U	W	3-2		8
4 SEP.8	(H)	BLACKBURN R	W	3-0	1G	8
5 SEP. 10	(H)	TRANMERE R	W	2-0		8
6 SEP. 17	(A)	CHESTERFIELD	L	1-3		8
7 SEP.24	(H)	SWANSEA T	D	1-1	1G	8
8OCT.1	(A)	BRADFORD	L	1-3		8
9 OCT.8	(H)	MANCHESTER C	W	3-1	1G	8
10OCT.15	(A)	SOUTHAMPTON	L	3-4		8
12 OCT.29	(A)	SHEFFIELD U	D	0-0		8
13NOV.5	(H)	NEWCASTLE U	L	0-2		8
14NOV.12	(A)	WEST BROM A	L	1-5		8
15NOV.19	(H)	NORWICH C	W	7-0		8
16NOV.26	(A)	LUTON T	W	5-1		8
17DEC.3	(H)	PLYMOUTH A	L	1-2		8
18 DEC. 10	(A)	NOTTINGHAM F	D	3-3	1G	8
19DEC.17	(H)	BURNLEY	W	4-1	1G	8
20 DEC.24	(A)	BURY	W	3-2	1G	8
21 DEC.27	(H)	FULHAM	W	5-1	1G	8
22 JAN. 1	(H)	WEST HAM U	L	1-4		8
23 JAN.2	(A)	BLACKBURN R	W	4-2	1G	8
FA3 JAN.7	(H)	YEOVIL	D	1-1	1G	8
FAR JAN. 12	(A)	YEOVIL	W	2-1		8
24 JAN. 14	(A)	TRANMERE R	W	4-1		8
FA4 JAN.21	(H)	CHESTER	D	1-1		8
FAR JAN.25	(A)	CHESTER	D	1-1	1G	8
25 JAN.28	(A)	SWANSEA T	W	1-0		8
FA2R JAN 30	(MANCH)	CHESTER	W	2-0	1G	8
26 FEB.4	(H)	BRADFORD	W	2-0	1G	8
FAS FEB. 11	(A)	CHELSEA	D	1-1	1G	8
FAR FEB. 13	(H)	CHELSEA	D	0-0		8
FAR FEB. 18	(H)	SOUTHAMPTON	W	2-0		8
FA2R FEB.20	HIGHBURY	CHELSEA	L	1-3		8
28 FEB.25	(A)	COVENTRY C	L	0-1		8
29 MAR.4	(H)	SHEFFIELD U	W	1-0		8
30 MAR. 11	(A)	NEWCASTLE U	L	1-2		8
31 MAR.18	(H)	WEST BROM A	W	2-1	1G	8
32 MAR.20	(H)	CHESTERFIELD	D	0-0		8
33 MAR.25	(A)	NORWICH C	D	2-2	1G	8
34 APR. 1	(H)	LUTON.T	W	4-1	1G	8
35 APR.7	(A)	MILLWALL	L	0-2		8
36 APR 8	(H)	NOTTINGHAM F	D	1-1	1G	8

1939-40 (DIV.2.)

1 AUG.26	(A)	LUTON T	L	2-0		8
1 AUG.28	(H)	BARNSLEY	W	3-1		8

EAST MIDLANDS REG. DIV.

6.NOV.4	(A)	GRIMSBY T	L	2-3		8
7.NOV.11	(H)	CHESTERFIELD	L	4-0		8

LEAGUE NORTH CUP

24 APR.20	(A)	LEEDS UNITED	L	3-6		8
25 APR.27	(H)	LEEDS UNITED	W	3-2		8

1940-41 (NORTH REG. LEAGUE)

5.OCT.5	(A)	MIDDLESBROUGH	L	4-5	2G	8
6.OCT.12	(H)	BARNSLEY	D	2-2		8
9.NOV.2	(H)	MIDDLESBROUGH	W	6-3	2G	8
10 NOV.2	(A)	DONCASTER R	D	4-4		8
13 NOV.30	(H)	BRADFORD	W	4-3		8
14 DEC.7	(A)	ROTHERHAM U	L	0-1		8
20 JAN.25	(A)	NEWCASTLE U	L	1-7		8
LWCP FEB.8	(H)	YORK C	W	2-1	1G	8
21 MAR.1	(A)	BARNSLEY	L	1-7		8
25 MAR.29	(H)	BURNLEY	L	0-2		8

1941-42 F.L. (NORTH)

9 OCT.25	(H)	SHEFFIELD U	L	1-3		8
10 NOV.1	(A)	SHEFFIELD U	D	3-3	3G	8
11 NOV.8	(A)	MANSFIELD T	L	0-4		8
13 NOV.22	(H)	CHESTERFIELD	D	1-1	1G	8
15 DEC.6	(A)	BARNSLEY	L	3-4	1G	8
18 DEC.25	(A)	NEWCASTLE U	W	4-2	2G	8
19 DEC.27	(H)	EVERTON	L	0-3		8
21 JAN.10	(H)	BRADFORD C	L	0-1		8

1942-43 (F.L. NORTH)

1 AUG.29	(A)	DONCASTER	W	3-1	1G	8
4 SEP.19	(A)	ROTHERHAM U	D	2-2	1G	8
5 SEP.26	(H)	BRADFORD	W	1-0		8
7 OCT.10	(A)	GRIMSBY T	L	0-2		8
8 OCT.10	(H)	GRIMSBY T	W	2-0		8
9 OCT.17	(H)	BARNSLEY	W	5-1	2G	8
10 OCT.31	(A)	BARNSLEY	W	3-0	1G	8
11 MAR.7	(H)	MANSFIELD T	W	9-1	3G	8
12 MAR.14	(A)	MANSFIELD T	W	10-2	3G	8
13 MAR.21	(A)	NOTTS C	D	2-2		8
14 MAR.28	(H)	NOTTS C	W	3-1	3G	8
17 DEC.19	(H)	SHEFFIELD U	W	4-0	2G	8
18 DEC.25	(A)	SHEFFIELD U	L	0-3		8

LEAGUE CUP (NORTH)

19 DEC.26	(H)	LINCOLN C	W	4-3	3G	8
20 JAN.2	(A)	LINCOLN C	W	3-0	1G	8
21 JAN.9	(A)	NOTTINGHAM F	D	1-1		8
22 JAN.16	(H)	NOTTINGHAM F	D	1-1		8
23 JAN.23	(H)	ROTHERHAM U	W	3-2	3G	8
24 JAN.30	(A)	ROTHERHAM U	D	1-1		8
25 FEB.6	(A)	SHEFFIELD U	L	1-3	1G	8
26 FEB.13	(H)	SHEFFIELD U	W	8-2	3G	8
28 FEB.27	(A)	GRIMSBY T	W	2-1		8
30 MAR.13	(A)	BRADFORD C	D	1-1	1G	8
31 MAR.20	(A)	NOTTINGHAM F	L	0-1		8
32 MAR.27	(H)	NOTTINGHAM F	W	5-1	1G	8
33 APR.3	(H)	SHEFFIELD U	W	3-2	2G	8
34 APR.10	(A)	SHEFFIELD U	D	0-0		8
35 APR.17	(H)	YORK C	W	3-0	2G	8
36 APR.24	(A)	YORK C	D	1-1		8
37 MAY.1	(A)	BLACKPOOL	D	2-2	1G	8
38 MAY.8	(H)	BLACKPOOL	L	1-2	1G	8

1943-44 (F.L.NORTH)

1 AUG.28	(A)	BARNSLEY	L	1-3	1G	8
2 SEP.4	(H)	BARNSLEY	W	3-1	1G	8
3 SEP.11	(H)	DONCASTER R	D	2-2		8
4 SEP.18	(A)	DONCASTER R	L	1-3	1G	8
5 SEP.25	(A)	BRADFORD	L	1-3	1G	8
7 OCT.9	(A)	ROTHERHAM U	L	1-5	1G	8
8 OCT.16	(H)	ROTHERHAM U	D	1-1		8
9 OCT.23	(H)	GRIMSBY T	L	2-3	1G	8
10 OCT.30	(A)	GRIMSBY T	W	3-1	1G	8
11 NOV.6	(A)	MANSFIELD T	W	2-0	1G	8
15 DEC.4	(H)	CHESTERFIELD	W	5-0	GG	8
17 DEC.18	(H)	SHEFFIELD U	W	0-2		8
18 DEC.25	(A)	SHEFFIELD U	D	1-1	1G	8
19 DEC.27	(A)	CHESTERFIELD	W	2-0	1G	8
25FEB.12	(H)	LEICESTER C	L	0-3		8
26 FEB.19	(H)	NOTTS C	W	2-0		9
32 APR.1	(A)	LINCOLN C	L	1-2		8
38 MAY.6	(A)	YORK C	L	3-4		9

1944-45 (F.L.NORTH)

1 AUG.26	(H)	SHEFFIELD U	D	1-1		8
2 SEP.2	(A)	SHEFFIELD U	W	1-0		8
6 SEP.30	(A)	CHESTERFIELD	L	2-5	1G	8
9 OCT.21	(H)	ROTHERHAM U	W	1-0	1G	8
11 NOV.4	(A)	LINCOLN C	W	3-0	3G	8
15 DEC.2	(H)	NOTTINGHAM F	W	2-1		8
16 DEC.9	(A)	NOTTINGHAM F	L	0-1	1G	9
18 DEC.23	(H)	BARNSLEY	W	5-0	1G	10
19 DEC.25	(H)	SHEFFIELD U	L	1-2		8
23 JAN.20	(H)	ROTHERHAM U	L	4-1		8
25 FEB.3	(A)	DONCASTER R	W	3-1	1G	8
26 FEB.10	(H)	DONCASTER R	L	1-6		8
37 APR.21	(H)	BRADFORD	W	3-1	2G	8
39 MAY.5	(A)	BARNSLEY	D	3-3	1G	8
42 MAY.19	(A)	SHEFFIELD U	W	3-1	1G	8
43 MAY.26	(H)	SHEFFIELD U	W	4-2	1G	8

1945-46 (F.L. NORTH)

1 AUG.25	(H)	SUNDERLAND	W	6-3	3G	8
3 SEP.8	(A)	SHEFFIELD U	W	3-1	1G	8
5 SEP.15	(H)	SHEFFIELD U	W	2-1	2G	8
6 SEP.22	(H)	MIDDLESBROUGH	W	2-1		8
9 OCT.13	(H)	STOKE C	W	1-0		8
12 NOV.3	(A)	BLACKPOOL	L	1-5		8
13 NOV.10	(H)	BLACKPOOL	W	3-2	2G	8
18 DEC.15	(H)	BLACKBURN R	D	1-1		8
19 DEC.22	(A)	BLACKBURN R	L	1-2		8
20 DEC.25	(A)	BRADFORD	L	2-3	1G	8
21 DEC.26	(H)	BRADFORD	W	3-0	2G	8
23 JAN.1	(A)	NEWCASTLE U	L	0-2		8
FA3 JAN.5	(A)	MANSFIELD	D	0-0		8
FA5 JAN.11	(A)	STOKE C	D	0-0		8
34 MAR.20	(A)	BOLTON W	L	1-2		8
35 APR.1	(H)	BOLTON W	D	0-0		8
36 APR.6	(A)	PRESTON NE	W	1-0	1G	10
37 APR.13	(H)	PRESTON NE	W	2-0	2G	10
38 APR.20	(A)	MANCHESTER U	L	0-4		10
39 APR.22	(A)	LEEDS U	W	1-0		10
40 APR.23	(H)	LEEDS U	W	2-0	1G	10
41 APR.27	(H)	MANCHESTER U	W	1-0	1G	10
42 MAY.4	(H)	NEWSCASTLE U	L	2-3	1G	10

1946-47 (DIV.2.)

1 AUG.31	(A)	LUTON T	L	1-4	1G	8
2 SEP.2	(H)	BARNSLEY	L	2-4		8
3 SEP.7	(H)	PLYMOUTH A	W	2-1	1G	8
4 SEP.9	(A)	BARNSLEY	L	4-1	1G	8
5 SEP.14	(A)	LEICESTER C	W	5-3	2G	8
6 SEP.16	(H)	FULHAM	D	1-1	1G	8
7 SEP.21	(H)	CHESTERFIELD	L	0-1		8

SCORING STATISTICS

FOR SHEFFIELD WEDNESDAY

	APP.	GOALS	DIV.	POS.
1934-35	1	1	1	10
1935-36	5	0	1	8
1936-37	29	5	1	4/10, 23/8, 1/9. 1/7
1936-37	1	1	FA CUP	8
1937-38	29	7	2	2/10.1/7,26/8
1938-39	37	15	2	8
1938-39	8	4	FA CUP	8
1939-40	2	0	2	8
1939-40	2	0	EASTMID	8
1940-41	9	7	NORTHREG	8
1940-41	1	1	LEAGUE WAR CUP	8
1941-42	8	7	NORTH	8
1942-43	14	16	NORTH	8
1942-43	18	19	NORTH	8
1943-44	13	11	NORTH	8
1943-44	5	1	NORTH	2/9, 3/8
1944-45	8	6	NORTH	6/8, 1/9, 1/10
1944-45	8	6	NORTH	8
1945-46	21	17	NORTH	14/8, 7/10
1945-46	2	0	FA CUP	8
1946-47	7	6	2	8
	228	130		

FOR SUNDERLAND F.C (Joined 14th October, 1946)

1946-47	30	17	1
1946-47	1	1	FA CUP
1947-48	23	6	1
1948-49	29	9	1
1948-49	2	1	FA CUP
	85	34	

FOR LINCOLN CITY (Joined 14th October, 1949)

1949-50	8	5	3 (NORTH)
1949-50	1/9	0/3	FA CUP

FOR ENGLAND

20th MAY 1937	v	FINLAND	(A)	8-0	1 GOAL
14th MAY 1938	v	GERMANY	(A)	6-3	2 GOALS
21st MAY 1938	v	SWITZERLAND	(A)	1-2	
22nd OCT 1938	v	WALES	(A)	2-4	

FOR ENGLAND FOOTBALL LEAGUE

21st SEPT 1943	v	IRELAND	(A)	6-2	1 GOAL

FOR ENGLAND ARMY

20th FEB 1938	v	SCOTLAND ARMY	(A)	7-0	4 GOALS

Note: All of these games were played away, what a shame for the English fans.

FOR SHEFFIELD WEDNESDAY - TOUR MATCH

1946 CLOSE SEASON	v	I.F.K. MALMO, SWEDEN	(A)	9-2	3 GOALS

IMPORTANT DATES

Jackie Robinson Born	August 10th 1917	
Played V. W.B.A.	April 22nd, 1935	17 years, 8 months
England Trial	March 17th, 1937	19 years, 9 months
v Finland	May 20th, 1937	19 years, 9 months
v Germany	May 14th, 1938	20 years, 9 months
v Switzerland	May 21st, 1938	20 years, 9 months
Married to Lillian Casson	October 12th, 1938	21 years, 2 months
v Wales	October 22nd, 1938	21 years, 2 months
Daughter Yvonne Born	April 16th, 1939	21 years, 8 months
Daughter Jacqueline Born	May 19th, 1950	32 years, 9 months
Son Raymond Born	July 3rd, 1952	34 years, 11 months
Jackie Robinson Died	July 30th, 1972	54 years, 11 months

ACKNOWLEDGMENTS

I would like to thank Mr. Geoff Hulley for giving me support for this book on behalf of Sheffield Wednesday Football Club.

I would also like to express my thanks and gratitude to Mr. Paul License of The Sheffield Star newspapers for allowing me to reproduce photographs and cuttings from my many scrapbooks. Without this my book may not have been so well illustrated or interesting.

Thanks to my friend Ray Smith who dug into his own memorabilia to find a few photos that helped give a more detailed account of Jackie Robinson.

A big thank you to Michael Liversidge and his colleagues at Pickard Communication on the splendid publication of The Jackie Robinson Story.

Many thanks to my family and friends for all their support and encouragement.

Last but not least, a big thank you to Pam Penistone, who has been with me all the way in this book, running around, gathering information and spending hours on the computer. At times when things were not going too well, she supported me. Without encouragement from Pam, I may not have finished this book.

Eric Brodie, 2004